The Agreeable World
of
Wallace Arnold

The Agreeable World
of
WALLACE ARNOLD

edited by
Craig Brown
illustrations by Willie Rushton

FOURTH ESTATE · *London*

First published in Great Britain in 1990 by
Fourth Estate Ltd
289 Westbourne Grove
London W11 2QA

British Library Cataloguing in Publication Data
Arnold Wallace
the agreeable world of Wallace Arnold
I. Title. II. Brown, Craig
828.91407

ISBN 1-87218-032-9

Typeset in Bembo by York House Typographic Ltd, Hanwell W7
Printed and bound by Clays Ltd, Bungay, Suffolk

Epigraph:
'**Wit** *n*. **1** (in *sing* or *pl*) intelligence; quick understanding
(*has quick wits; a nimble wit*). **2 a** the unexpected, quick, and
humorous combining or contrasting of ideas of expressions
(*conversation sparkling with wit*); **b** the power of giving
intellectual pleasure by this. **3** a person possessing such a
power, esp. a cleverly humorous person.'
The Concise Oxford Dictionary

A good mind possesses a kingdom.
SENECA

We come nearest to the great when we are great in humility.
RABINRATH TAGORE

To my old friend and quaffing-partner,
Napier Miles esq.

CONTENTS

INTRODUCTION

My thanks are due to Lord Weidenfeld for first suggesting this lengthy project during a brief hiatus in a conversation in spring 1959; to Mr Graham Greene, for his permission to quote from extensive private conversations, many of them deeply embarrassing, some confirming one's very worst impressions of him; to the late Ayatollah and Mrs Khomeini, for many happy hours on the golf course; to HRH Queen Elizabeth the Queen Mother, for her permission to ransack the Clarence House archives for any information that could prove deleterious to the reputations of her close relations; to the people of Liverpool for their characteristically generous help in the preparation of the chapter pertaining to the advances achieved by their fair city following my extensive efforts on their behalf; to Bubbles, Lady Rothermere, for her general encouragement, wise counsel and contagious sense of fun; to Mr J. Enoch Powell for many delightful evenings spent on the razzle in Monte Carlo – and beyond(!); to Conservative Central Office, and in particular the Prime Minister, for allowing me time off in order to 'polish up' the essays and 'bons mots' herein contained; to General and Mrs Manuel Noriega for many an agreeable evening reminiscing in the snug bar of the Garrick; to Miss Barbara Skelton, for her permission to quote extensively from her literary reminiscence *All Man: My Years with Wallace Arnold*; and to all those in the fields of royalty, enterprise, politics and the arts who would wish to be mentioned but for whom I can find neither the time nor the effort. Finally, my thanks are due to my long-suffering secretary, HRH Prince Edward, who has done a great deal of the donkey-work for virtually no reward whatsoever, and to Sir Roy Strong, for simply being himself.

> *Wallace Arnold*
> *Balmoral*
> *Monte Carlo*
> *Washington*
> *Firenze*
> *Londres*
> *May 1959 – August 1990*

ABSENT FRIENDS

Fond memories of a young mortician

For Arnold, reviewing is never simply a matter of describing and assessing the contents of a book. He is far more interested in the artist behind the words, especially if he knows him socially. He demonstrates his skill at character analysis in this wide-ranging review of Absent Friends, *a book of reminiscences of acquaintances by a Mr Geoffrey Wheatcroft published in 1989, but now, like the acquaintances themselves, sadly remaindered.*

W.A.

Page three(!) of this agreeable, highly civilised tome contains bitter news indeed for the many friends and admirers of Mr Wheatcroft. Introducing his *pot pourri* of portraits of the recently departed, Wheaters declares that 'they form a sort of autobiography (I am not sure what sort)', adding, alas and alack, 'not that I ever wanted or want to write such a thing'. Grave news, indeed, for all lovers of the printed word. If there is one volume my extensive library sorely lacks, it must surely be 'I, Wheatbags: The Life and Times of Geoffrey Wheatcroft'. It is my most earnest hope that readers of this admirable journal, every bit as much aggrieved as I at so tragic a loss to English letters, will be goaded to put pen to paper and write to Mr Wheatcroft, begging him to think again. I feel sure that if as many as three such letters fall upon his mat, our most noted *écriviste* will change his mind in the proverbial jiffy, rattling off a good ten thousand words on Mummy and Daddy Wheaters before nipping off for a hearty luncheon with close friends.

Until that day comes, we must remain satisfied with such glimpses of the real Wheatcroft as we can espy amidst the characteristically self-effacing leaves of these reminiscences of the deceased. How vividly his pen brings the notable — if dead! – coves to life! With a pithy phrase, the author can summon the dear departed into our very drawing-rooms (or – dread word! – 'lounges'). Pray allow me to offer a few examples of this almost magical ability. *On Philip Larkin*: 'He admired me, yes, but I sometimes feel that, deep within his soul, there remained some small jealousy at my *savoir faire* and way with words. Nevertheless, a by no means inconsiderable poet.' *On Sir A.J.Ayer*: 'I now think that he was always delighted to see me, for he was a restless fellow, always on the lookout for an intellectual equal. Much of what he believed was frankly hogwash, but it should never be said of him that he failed to find solace in my amusing *reveries*, on cricket, young ladies, and what, for want of a better word, one might term "life".' *On Hugh Fraser*: 'A clubman, a gentleman and something of a card, blessed with the dashing good looks of a knight of old, gallant, salty, honourable: this was how Hugh came to see me over the many long years of our friendship. To do him justice, his own character, too, was not without interest.'

After wallowing in these delightful *vignettes*, the reader (I place the aforesaid noun in the singular, but, who knows, this very review might send sales rocketing into the plural – fingers crossed!) will desperately want to know more about this latter-day Boswell, this erudite man-about-town who seems equally at home in the bars of Fleet Street as in the afternoon drinking-clubs of Soho. How, this mythical reader may wonder, did this Wheatcroft fellow come to conquer the many grave disadvantages so cruelly foisted upon him by his Maker to emerge at the very forefront of contemporary letters, an acknowledged authority on the inner lives of his equals? It is a tale of courage and nobility, a lifelong struggle against the odds; and it is a tale that deserves to be told as only Wallace Arnold knows how.

'Geoffrey Fido Wheatcroft was born in 1945. He read Modern History as a Scholar of New College and studied typography on coming down from Oxford.' Thus begins the author's endearingly modest dust-jacket 'blurb' (vulgar word!). 'His pallid complexion and rubbery features,' continues said 'blurb', 'found him drawn ineluctably to the only trade compatible with his aptitudes and habits of life, and, in 1973, he became an apprentice mortician at one of the most prestigious mortuaries in South-East London. In 1981, he was elected a member of the Royal Society of Morticians and Corpse Disposal Operatives, earning the Society's Silver Medal in 1986. He also dabbles in freelance journalism, having contributed to the *Sunday Telegraph* and *Options* magazine.'

The pieces in Geoffrey's engaging new collection are drawn largely from his life in the mortuary, for it was here that he first met the vast majority of those whom he takes such pleasure in describing. As a young morti-cian, he had the great good fortune to find himself alone in a room with the corpse of Bertrand Russell, arguably (delicious adverb!) the greatest British philosopher of the 20th century. Russell, he reports, 'sat quite still and silent while I entertained him with a blow-by-blow account of Freddie Trueman's first century at Lord's, and remained enraptured whilst I took issue with him over his feeble-minded support for the ludicrous shena-nigans of the so-called "Ban the Bomb" movement. His politics were not mine, as he would have been the first to agree, but we had much in common, including a canny sense of humour, a love of Mathematics, and, if truth be told, something of an eye for the fairer sex. "Bertie" I remarked as he sat there, enraptured, "have I ever explained to you my position on Napoleon? No? Well, I do not subscribe to the theory that 'Boney' was . . . " and I proceeded to hold him spellbound for two hours with my views on this much-maligned historical figure.'

Other corpses, many of them eminent, were soon to follow, and Geoffrey treated them all with his customary courtesy and respect, while steadfastly refusing to 'water down' his own, far from uninteresting, point of view. Having encountered these renowned, albeit deceased, figures he would nip home to his *pied à terre* to fill his notebooks with the many *bons mots* he had uttered in their presence, and this wholly delightful book is the happy result of his labours. Whether discussing the Northern Ireland situation with Dame Margaret Rutherford or pondering the overrated *oeuvre* of Jean Luc Godard with Harold Macmillan, Wheaters maintains an unflagging interest in his own opinions, and is always prepared to 'hold forth' while his eager disciples sit rooted to the spot.

And so to today. Wheatbags is an all-too-familiar figure in the hurly-burly of Literary London, but it would be a mistake to imagine that his attendance at any party, no matter how small, is ever purely social. Those who do not know the man well assume that his frequent horizontal appearances upon drawing-room and even bathroom floors are perchance connected to a penchant for a tipple or two, but far from it. Wheaters brings a mortician's eye to every social occasion, and he can boast quite truthfully an ability to measure any man or woman for the coffin at thirty paces. His frequent trips to the floorboards are a testament to his unfailing professionalism, for he will always size up a man's feet before the final estimate is completed. A consummate *artiste*, methinks, but how one yearns for a tome that tells us more about the man himself.

AMIS PERE

(1) In which an old friendship is renewed with the Old Devil (!)

The Arnold commonplace book is in many ways influenced by the journals of the Goncourt Brothers. Witness here how he transmutes a 'slice of life' – luncheon with Kingsley Amis – into literature simply by noticing the minutiae of the great novelist's speech patterns, mannerisms and ideas. Amis himself was reportedly delighted by this deft, deceptively simple portrait.

W.A.

The maestro of the belly-laugh leant back in his seat, taking another puff on his cigar as he wiped his Steak-and-Oyster starter from his chin, and beckoned the waiter to top up his pint mug of Black Velvet with some more Chateauneuf-du-Pape. 'And shove another Bloody Mary in there as well,' he said, placing a few bread rolls in his pocket for safe keeping. 'And give the whole thing a decent stir. Tastes revolting if it's not stirred. No-one stirs anything these days. Service? Bloody hell. That's a laugh.'

Kingsley Amis is back on stinging form with his new novel, *Dreadful Old Bags*, another blisteringly funny sideswipe at everything modern and feminine. Arnold and Amis go back yonks, so I had invited the old devil to the restaurant of his choice to celebrate publication. He had taken up my invitation by booking himself a suite at the Connaught for a couple of weeks. When I walked into the dining-room, he was obviously delighted to see me, hastily pouring his rice pudding into an inside pocket 'to keep it warm'.

'What did you say your name was? What? What?' he greeted me, ever the consummate ironist. I reminded him, and he countered with a superbly executed ironic grimace. Once I had finished laughing, we got down to brass tacks. 'Kingsley, old boy', I began, 'we're both great admirers of each other's *oeuvres*, and I was wondering if I might bother you with one or two awful questions for the *Spec*?'

'Could murder a leg of lamb', he responded. 'And I mean *lamb*. Not that stringy stuff they serve these days. This could do with a top-up too.' He raised his empty mug in the direction of a waiter. 'Needs more – what's the stuff? – sherry. And a touch of Calvados. And heavy on the Armagnac.'

'Have your views on women changed since the early days, would you say?'

'Women? Women! Don't talk to me about women. Now where's that Chateaubriand I ordered?' Vintage Amis!

From women, our talk turned to poetry. I told him how much I had admired the lines in his recent poem, 'Crappy Codswallop', in which he spoke of 'An awful load of tosh / Like Beckett and Joyce / And all that bosh'. What was he reading at the moment?

'What am I eating? What? What? Tastes like Dover Sole mucked about with some damnfool sauce. Bloody awful.'

And where did he stand on God? I have always been fascinated by God, and vice versa, but I wondered if Kingsley was a believer.

'Bloody sick-making. You ask for a leg of lamb and does it come? Does it hell.'

I told him how amused I had been by his masterly-description of a female social worker in his early novel *Creeps in Bras* as 'heavily moustachioed and spouting claptrap', and how I found this portrait strangely compassionate.

'Piss off' he replied, 'and pick up the bill on the way out.'

(2)In which the Old Devil entrusts a manuscript to his old quaffing-partner!

*K*ingsley Amis's two articles 'Sod the Public' and 'Sod the Public II', devastating critiques of the worst aspects of modern society printed in alphabetical order, had proved most agreeable to the Spectator readership. So it came as an honour to Arnold when he vouchsafed 'Sod the Public III' into his hands.

W.A.

'Loved your piece in the *Spec* the week before last, Kingsley.' I had managed to corner the King at a literary gathering of the type at which he and I tend to be Guests of Honour. 'Eh? Wassat? Who the hell are you?' he replied, employing his standard greeting to me, a joke that goes back yonks, and which we both enjoy.

' "Sod the Public II",' I reminded him, 'Excellent. Said what needs to be said.'

From out of his pocket he pulled an original Amis manuscript, entitled 'Sod the Public III'. 'Take it,' he said, 'but only on condition you push off, you silly farting pansy.' Vintage Amis! Chuckling gamely, I 'pushed off', as it were, original manuscript in hand. And this was how I came to be able to bring you another masterpiece from that delectable pen:

SOD THE PUBLIC III
FRESH VEGETABLES: This ghastly stuff is foisted on

the public by restaurateurs anxious to impress the Arts Council, probably in hot pursuit of some 'grant' or other. Where can you get a decent tinned peach these days? Or a decent bit of Mother's Pride? Oh, no, of course we can't have *that* – it's far too popular, and might please the public.

TROUSERS: In the good old days, a pair of trousers was designed to be comfortable to the wearer, but now they always make them too tight.

FLOWERS: Smelly, inedible, no good for anything. The only stuff worse is grass, livid green and often damp. Thinks it bloody owns the countryside.

OTHER PEOPLE: Never say anything of the remotest interest. No doubt they think they are being 'entertaining' or 'adventurous' in opening their mouths. Fat lot they know.

MUSIC: The purpose of all music seems to be 'Sod the tone-deaf' just as the purpose of all art seems to be 'Sod the blind'. By playing only for people who can 'appreciate' music, musicians are keeping it in the club and tweaking their noses at the general public. And the same goes for composers.

SUNSHINE: Another of the lazy buggers. In the old days, you could bank on the sun shining all day, regardless of season, but now it's only in the summer months and sometimes not even then. Even when it's willing to bloody shine, the damn thing gets in your eyes, so that it's impossible to read a decent book (or would be, if there were such a thing) without squinting or going indoors.

MIRRORS: Used to be perfectly all right, showing a perfectly decent and engaging young man. Now only show grumpy buffoons. Yet another example of the slovenly, contemptuous attitude for the needs of those it serves.

The list goes on for another fifty pages or more,

encompassing virtually every peril of modern life, from the electric light bulb to toothpaste, all polished off with the King's incomparable style and wit. Alas, no more room for them this week, but, even in this minor way, I'm only too delighted to have acted as Kingsley's Bosworth.

'The maestro of the belly-laugh leant back in his seat.'

AMIS FILS

Kingsley's son, Martin, is, alas, a very different kettle of fish!

*A*rnold *has set many a young scribe on the first rung of success, and has long been generous with his tips on punctuation, intellectual rigour and personal hygiene. But there will always be the one rotten apple. In this moving and occasionally bitterly upsetting fragment of autobiography, Arnold recounts, in all-too-graphic detail, his encounter with the young Martin Amis.*

W.A.

In the early 1970s (dread decade!) I had the great good fortune to earn my crust as Motoring Editor of that perennially chucklesome journal, *Punch*. Knowing not a little about those vehicular four-wheelers known as cars, and a fair amount, too, about the tricky business of humour, I was ideally placed to edit half a dozen books in the *Punch* 'Humour of Motoring' series.

I mention all this not simply by way of awarding myself a few blasts on me old tuba, but to introduce a two-part reminiscence of the young Martin Amis. Ever keen to give a young spark a lift up on to the first step of the proverbial ladder, I had heard that my old quaffing-partner and fellow scribe Kingers had given birth to a stripling of a lad, fresh from college and mustard-keen to make his way in the World of Witty Wordsmiths.

With all due haste, I summoned the spotty-faced youngster to my cubby-hole to suggest he pen a tome entitled *The Humour of Motoring . . . in London*, with illustrations by Thelwell, the whole designed with the entertainment of the General Motorist in mind. Young Martin seemed over the moon with his first commission, not quite smiling, but at any rate smirking less ostentatiously for one or two minutes.

A month or two passed, and, one sunny morn, Mr Postie delivered the aforesaid manuscript to my (delightfully and characteristically chaotic!) desk. To be utterly frank, the first thing to strike me about this pile of typewritten sheets was quite how filthy it was: peculiar stains seemed smeared over nigh on every page, sometimes binding whole chapters together, so that one had to prise them apart with trusty paper-knife and a goodly dab of elbow grease. Without going into too much detail, I will simply say that the young *écriviste* had obviously been suffering from some form of heavy catarrh while setting pen to paper, combined, alas, with a tummy complaint. Other stains of a less readily identifiable hue clogged up pages 55–73, while an almost unwholesome amount of earwax made pages 132–89 virtually impregnable. Without being unnecessarily explicit, posterity obliges me to record that, noticing something of a bump between pages 14 and 15, I held the offending leaves over a boiling kettle and, within minutes, what should pop out but something my office secretary, a woman of advanced years, was quick to recognise as a 'condom' (dread word!).

Far from being a sideways look at the mirth of motoring, with previously agreed chapter titles such as 'If this is Tuesday, it must be Piccadilly!', the book concerned itself primarily with over-vivid descriptions of tramps 'letting off' in the back of stolen Cortinas, while Chapter Ten had been re-titled 'Sodomising Your Exhaust Pipe'. Needless to say, I realised there and then that asking HRH the Duke of Edinburgh to pen a brief but witty foreword was now out of the question.

* * *

As an old quaffing-partner of Amis *père*, I was most
anxious not to cross swords with young Martin, so I
decided to 'let him down gently', as it were, by issuing
him with an invitation to a *Punch* lunch. At that time
·the alas now sadly depleted tradition of the lunch was in
its veritable heyday, and each Thursday the dining-
room would throb with a galaxy of scribes, statesmen
and jesters to rival the Kennedy White House. On a
typical day, one would find oneself exchanging repartee with Miss Anita 'Just Loving You' Harris to one's
right and Miss Libby Purves to one's left, while lending
half an ear to the ticklish reminiscences of disastrous
family holidays (!) from Mr Hunter Davies opposite.

Having invited young Martin to bask in the reflected
glory of breaking bread with the stars, I planned to
whisper a polite thumbs-down to him o'er the non-
vintage port, surmising that, amidst the hurly-burly of
celebrity exchanging anecdote with celebrity, he would
good-heartedly shrug off the whole unfortunate
episode.

I remember well his entry into the illustrious dining-
room. The cream of *Punch* contributors was there –
Mike Parkinson, Uncle Bill Davis, Cyril Fletcher, the
lot – as well as a goodly sprinkling of external celebri-
ties of the calibre of Mr Roy Hudd, Miss Wendy Craig
and the immortal Mr Terry Scott. I had placed Martin
next to Lord Hailsham on the one side and, on the
other, the three Beverley Sisters, who insisted on sharing a single chair and would contentedly spoon soup
into one another's mouths by means of a closed-circuit
walkie-talkie system.

Amis *fils* was ushered in by our liveried manservant.
I recognised him at once. While the rest of us had had
the good grace to don black tie, he chose to wear odd
socks, a string vest soaked in last Tuesday's scrambled
egg, a pair of soiled underpants and, masquerading as a

makeshift tie, a hastily elongated 'tampon'. And little else. Repartee, I need hardly add, came to an abrupt halt.

'Aha!' I exclaimed, attempting to smooth things over. 'Amis *fils*! Most hearty of welcomes, dear boy! Take a pew and pray plunder our modest repast!'

'Whassis, then?' inquired Martin of Babs Beverley, pointing a grubby finger in the direction of his chicken broth. 'Liquid puke?'

Thereon, things went speedily downhill. Over the course of the meal, he compared Miss Craig to a screeching wombat, Mr Terry Scott to an over-inflated giblet and Lord Hailsham to a semi-castrated Pekinese. Ushering him out before pudding arrived, I informed him in no uncertain terms that he was most unsuitable to contribute to *Punch*, thereupon handing him back his manuscript and, in so doing, finding my right hand stained with a mixture of urine and saliva that not even three hearty scrubbings with Swarfega could wholly erase. I daresay his new tome is fashionable, smutty, 'with-it', etcetera, but it will be afforded no place at the Arnold bedside.

LORD BEAVERBROOK

Fond memories of 'The Beaver'

*D*uring the second half of the 1980s, Britain's national newspapers all moved away from their traditional home in Fleet Street. This caused Arnold to reflect on times past, on the characters he had known and on one magnetic figure in particular: the man they knew as 'The Beaver'. Note Arnold's telling use of the illuminating anecdote as a device for revealing character.

W.A.

Whither Fleet Street? The camaraderie felt by all those who toiled there has, I regret to say, disappeared, to be replaced by the 'word processor', the 'fax machine' and the drear skyscrapers of Docklands, the Isle of Dogs, Wapping or wherever. Young, up-and-coming journalists will never know what it is like to sup ale with the legendary figures of Fleet Street – Pisser Crabtree of the *Herald*, Gentleman Jack Bowles of the *News*, Stuffer Gould of the *Standard* – and to hear them at first hand regaling a mirth-filled watering-hole with hilarious anecdotes of their narrow escapes abroad, their immortal set-tos with the Beaver and high-jinks behind the war lines. Instead, they must remain content in a world bereft of the richness of the whisky bottle in the filing cabinet, the darts board behind the desk and the smelly sock in the bottom drawer, a world without character or poetry.

As the last national newspaper pulls up stumps from

the Street, my mind returns to those joyous far-off days. There are many names to remember, characters all. One thinks of Sickbag Stanley of the *Star*, who would puke into his top pocket every morning before dictating a word-perfect leader on the Suez crisis, or the equally legendary Smutty Corns, theatre critic of the *Chronicle*, who liked to boast that he had never seen a single play he had reviewed ('Affects one's judgement so, dear boy!!!'), or of old Stinker Harness, revered by one and all as the only man ever to drink three bottles of Scotch through a secret straw while interviewing Princess Grace of Monaco.

One would saunter into El Vino come teatime, there to see all these legendary figures issuing their latest rib-ticklers, many of them quite outrageous, I might say(!), to the young men and women who formed their coteries. Magical coves, magical days.

But a young whipper-snapper, with little more to offer than an avid eye for the absurd, a keen intelligence, an indomitable integrity and a wining manner, I was for some reason taken to their heart. These legends of the Street would allow the young Arnold to listen as they told their tales of the legends that had preceded them. It was an education no university could offer, and, now that I have become a legend myself, I always make a point of waylaying young scribblers to tell them, in my own hilariously idiosyncratic way, of these formative figures in my career as a writer and opinion-former. My only payment is their gratitude.

Beaverbrook seemed to have a special place in his heart for me. Others saw him as a monster, but I brought out the great magnanimity of the man. On the only occasion on which we actually met, he looked me straight in the eye and said – and I'll never forget the words – 'The lace of your left shoe is undone.' Needless to say, I've been dining out on that story ever since.

A BOOK REVIEW

The best critic always reveals a little of himself!

*M*r Ron Waugh, editor of the Literary Review, *would often buttonhole Arnold to review books for his little-read magazine. The most scrupulous of reviewers, Arnold always made a point of giving each and every book a cursory glance before sitting down to write about it. On this occasion, Mr Waugh sent him* May Week Was in June, *a second volume of autobiography by Mr Clive James.*

W.A.

Though essentially *un homme serieux*, I have, as is widely known, from time to time engaged myself in the act of the humorous composition. The light-hearted essay containing the jocular (and occasionally waspish!) *aperçu* has long been a *forte* of mine, and the list of my contributions to *Punch* magazine in my *Who's Who* entry – 'The Lighter Side of Spring-Cleaning' (May 1969), 'If It's Wednesday, It Must Be Margate!' (April 1964), 'Broom! Clunk! – A Sideways Look At Car Maintenance' (August 1959), 'Pardon My Swahili – Wallace Arnold Goes On His Hols' (August 1974), 'The Unfairer Sex – All You Ever Wanted To Know About Birds Of The Unfeathered Variety' (Christmas Number 1971), 'Chortle Awhile with . . . Wallace Arnold' (February 1978), 'Never Again! – Wallace Arnold Tries His Hand At The Bobsleigh' (September 1982), 'Excuse My Ear-Muffs – A Sane View of Today's Pop "Music"' (January 1968), 'Names That Make Me

Chuckle' (weekly series, June 1966–March 1983) – reads like a veritable compendium of post-war English (*very* English!) humour.

During all this time as the *doyen* of comic writers, I have, I freely admit, never found myself adverse to taking the occasional 'crack' at the British Trades Union Movement. As early as 1962, I had invented the marvellously ridiculous – yet in a strange way oddly touching – figure of Len Grunt, Convenor of the Allied Union of Loafers, Grumblers and Slugabeds, a character who swiftly found his place in that pantheon of richly comic, thoroughly English figures in our national literature which also includes the immortal Mr Pooter and many others, the immortal Mrs Pooter to name but one.

Mr Len Grunt(!), I need hardly remind readers of the *Literary Review*, was the archetypal Trades Unionist: uncultured, grubby, stubborn and hopelessly unrealistic, with something of a passion for champagne. Excellent! I daresay my wicked lampoon caused a rich variety of red faces in the TUC headquarters, but it afforded my devoted readers no end of innocent amusement, and might, in large part, be said to have contributed to the Conservative victories of 1970 and 1974.

All of which brings me neatly – and conveniently! – to the tome in hand. Few of those who do not possess the creative gift realise that a fictitious character may be built and moulded, crafted and polished from a tremendous variety of human beings whom the artist (dread word!) has encountered during the course of a long and full life. Though it would thus be fallacious to dismiss the immortal Mr Len Grunt as merely the carbon-copy of any one public figure, I can now reveal that he owed much to the author of *May Week Was In June*, namely Mr Clive Jenkins.

Said tome, is, I am led to believe, the third, and, as one might imagine(!) final volume in a trilogy detailing

the 'early years' of Mr Clive Jenkins' illustrious life. I
have, I regret to say, yet to manage either of the two
earlier volumes, but a deep and considered perusal of
the volume in question has yielded a good few sur-
prises. The trilogy ends as the author graduates from
Cambridge University, with his lifelong career in the
Trades Union Movement still lying ahead of him. But
there is many a surprise 'twixt flyleaves, for how many
of us would have guessed that the one-time General-
issimo of the ASTMS (Assortment of Sod The Man-
agement Scroungers – I jest!) was once the proud
possessor of a promising career as President of the
Cambridge Footlights?

Oddly enough, I too am a Past President of that
distinguished body of jesters and merrymakers *extraordinaire*, and my rib-tickling productions of the now-
legendary revues *Laughter Please, Maestro!* (1953), *It's a
Funny Old World!* (1954) and the pace-setting *Line Up
For a Leg-Pull!* (1955) are still spoken of in hushed tones
to this very day. Whisper it not in the Shires, but I have
been known to set dinner-tables a-roar with my word-
for-word recitals of my spoof Hamlet soliloquy. 'To
bee or not to bee', I begin, and then, after a wickedly
long pause during which the sense of expectation
amongst the audience is virtually tangible, I go into my
'Buzz Buzz Buzz, Yes I AM a little Bee!' routine,
waggling my elbows to and fro and pretending to be
the striped insect in question!! Needless to say, it has
them hooting every time. Encore, Wallace, Encore!

Why, I wonder, did Mr Clive Jenkins give up his
talent for student theatricals to pursue a lifelong career
in support of beer and sandwiches (not to mention the
odd glass of the fizzy stuff!)? Who knows, he might
have enjoyed a reputation as something of a wit and a
raconteur, a television 'personality' along the lines,
perhaps, of Mr Clive James.

Oddly enough, mention of the name of Mr Clive

James prompts me to cast a second glance at the tome in question, and I now notice that I have 'mixed up my Clives', the scribbler under review being by Mr James and not, I fear, Mr Jenkins. I wonder, though, if this really matters one jot? Many of my points still hold, or at least one or two, and I would venture to suggest that my 'Buzzy Bee' anecdote, never before seen in print, will be popping up shortly in all the anthologies, and will be 'doing the rounds' long after the names of James and Jenkins are forgotten, so all is not lost, by any manner of means!!

MISS (MS!) JULIE BURCHILL

Being the case against the shrill scrivener

With the true touch of the master, Arnold never allows his book reviews to slip into the mire of the impersonal. Here he relates the publication of an unsuitable novel by an equally unsuitable young female novelist to the far wider and deeper civilisation to be encountered by the gifted and the well-born at Sir Harold Acton's charming palazzo *in* Firenze.

W.A.

I feel quite sure that most people who know anything (three? four? I jest!) will know that as the dappled dew of May makes way for the juniper-clad glow of early June, the cream of British literary society heads west for *Firenze*, there to sojourn with Sir Harold Acton at that divine *palazzo* 'La Pietra'. It is a time for wry, witty, worldly conversation; it is a time for friendship; it is a time for reflection; but perhaps above all else, it is a time for *books*.

Let me aspire to the briefest pen-portrait of such a house party, so that those who, candidly, stand no chance of receiving an invitation this year, next year, sometime, ever, will be able to relish the crumbs dropped from the table of those of us upon whom fortune has seen fit to smile. Popping one's head around those lacquered doors on to the verandah at *petit dejeuner*, one might glimpse Dr Rowse fingering an old Graham Greene; beside the terrace fountain, Kenneth Rose will be reciting passages from his splendidly entertaining *The Wit of the Titled* to an enraptured gathering of local tradesmen and rustics; and – lo! – up there on the balcony, his head all but shrouded in the morning mist, whom should one espy but my Lord St John of Fawsley busily perusing an exciting young British novelist!

By the evening, we 'early birds' have been joined by the 'married couples', and our reading grows apace: John Julius is tackling the quietly amusing memoirs of an 18th-century cleric; Johnny Mortimer trades literary badinage with the estimable Sir Roy Strong; Antonia Pinter is genning up on the prose-poems of Daniel Ortega, and way down in the scullery, Harold P, never what one might call a 'mixer', is challenging the trusty staff to an arm-wrestling competition, but only after they have finished the washing-up. And over this redoubtable treasure-trove of cultural leaders presides the inimitable figure of Sir Harold himself, clad, more often than not, in jim-jams of the finest silk, highly polished 'platform' boots and his characteristic pom-pom, reciting for those of us at a loose end a selection from his excellent collection of verse, *Of Ponies and Peonies* (1941).

Following a sumptuous repast, our solitary pleasures become communal. Each guest is expected to come up with a 'little something' from his knapsack of literary gems for the delectation of the company therein assembled. A smidgin of Brontë is followed by a soupçon of Drabble; a favourite Johnson anecdote is exchanged for a wicked witticism from Firbank; Johnny Mortimer scintillates with a new story about the incorrigible Rumpole (*what* a character!). This, one finds oneself declaring annually, is Civilisation, and we, it gladdens me to acknowledge, are the Civilised!

It is with no little sadness, then, that I feel impelled to recount the sorry events that overtook yours truly during my stay with Sir Harold *cette année*. This act I

perform not from spite nor from resentment, but so
that others might learn. Those who are excluded from
such a glittering circle – I speak now principally of the
Editor of this journal – are too often hell-bent on
destroying the standing of those at its centre. I am now
possessed by severe doubts as to whether Sir Harold
will welcome me back next year, and through no fault
of my own. Thanks, Bron. Thanks a lot.

Allow me to take a deep breath and explain. I had
arrived with a large travelling suitcase choc-a-bloc with
tomes both plentiful and various, all scrupulously
selected to reflect my famously Catholic – yet occasionally idiosyncratic! – taste. Following dinner on the
night of my stay, while poor Kenneth Rose was paus-
ing briefly for breath as he entertained the assembled
company with a reading from his own *The Wisdom of
the Marchioness of Abercrombie*, Sir Harold took advantage of the *hiatus*, and, turning to me, fedora ever so
slightly askew, said, 'Might we now be blessed with a
little something from the Wondrous Wallace?'

Amidst many an encouraging chuckle, I piped up
that Sir H had caught me 'on the hop'. Little realising
that I would be 'called', as it were, I had left my tome-
filled bag at the foot of my bed. Swiftly excusing
myself with undoubted ease and charm, I leapt the
marble stairs two-at-a-time. Reaching the main land-
ing, I could hear the distinctive tones of Kenneth Rose
attempting to 'bag' my spot, as it were, with what he
described as 'a few paragraphs' from his recent *Darling
Duchesses*. If I failed to act fast, I had no doubt that my
opportunity to enthral the gathering with my own
renderings from literature would be lost for ever. I thus
scooted with all haste into my bedroom, and, without
so much as turning on the light, plunged my hand into
the aforesaid bag, pulling out the very first volume
upon which I stumbled.

Hurtling myself downstairs with unprecedented

'The eyes of the civilised world were upon me.'

gusto, I arrived back in the drawing room in the nick of
time. Kenneth had just embarked upon his oration.
'The philanthropy of the British aristocracy has long
been renowned the world over,' he began.

Alas for dear Kenneth, my re-entry encouraged Sir
Harold to interject. 'Aha! The Return of the Artful
Arnold!' he exclaimed. Turning to Kenneth, he added,
'If you would be so good, Kenneth, as to read that to
yourself some other time, I think we are all awash with
excitement to discover with what literary *bonbon* Wallace has chosen to entertain us!'

The eyes of the civilised world were upon me as I
gazed for the first time at the book upon which my
hand had alighted with such haste. It was a novel I had
never read, by a woman of whom I had never heard,
the unknown *oeuvre* having been foisted upon me by
the irresponsible editor of the prestigious *Literary
Review* as being 'very much your sort of thing, Wally'.
It would never do, of course, to admit to my host and
fellow guests that I had no knowledge whatsoever of
the work in my hand, so I decided, there and then, to,
as it were, 'bluff it out.'

'Thank you for that kind introduction, Harold', I
said, for we have been on Christian name terms for
yonks. 'I have with me a book by – by – by' (at this
point I cast a stealthy eye to the dustjacket) 'by one Julie
Burchill, a sensitive young novelist, who is, I feel, erm,
erm, doing no more and no less than erm, erm, re-
inventing our very language and culture, erm, erm, in a
way that is both, erm, life-enhancing and erm, erm, yes
– paradoxical.'

'Mmmm. Paradoxical' an appreciative whisper
rushed around the finely-carpeted room. With my
famous 'second sense', I could perceive instinctively
that the interest of my audience had been awakened.

Now, it is not done at these *soirées chez Acton* to
blunder into a book at Chapter One, as this might raise

the suspicion amongst one's fellows that one possessed insufficient taste to select a particularly haunting passage from the work in question. Thus, I craftily pulled the said tome open a few pages in.

'I trust that you will all find this passage both moving, and, above all, erm, erm, plangent,' I said.

'Mmmm. Plangent' echoed the distinguished gathering. I had them in the palm of my hand. After a suitably dramatic pause, I plunged in at the first paragraph on the page.

'*Ever since Susan Street could remember,*' I began, allowing the warm expectation of a well-honed trip down memory lane to seep through my enraptured audience. '*Ever since Susan Street could remember,*' I repeated, and, from the glow in Roy's eyes, I could tell that there was much warmth in his heart for the trinkets of childhood memories: picnics o'er moss-cloaked glens, piggybacks for Mr Teddy, steam pud with lashings of custard, and so forth.

'*Ever since Susan Street could remember,*' I continued, '*men were launching themselves like ground-to-air missiles at your groin with their tongues hanging out the second after they'd first shaken hands with you.*'

There followed a stunned silence, punctuated only by a high-pitched cough from somewhere deep in the throat of Sir Roy Strong. John Julius began to untie and tie his shoes in quick succession. Antonia looked frankly aghast. I had to think fast.

'So sorry,' I blurted. 'Wrong passage. Silly Wallace! Ha!' I flipped the leaves ever onwards until my eyes were caught by what seemed to be a far more charming passage, and all around breathed a sigh of quiet relief.

'*The two girls were into their stride now, reaching a plateau beyond mere professional pride,*' I intoned. I had already drawn a rich smile from Norman Stevas.

'Adore girls' school stories,' he enthused. 'Always have, always will. More, maestro, more!'

'Two dears on a hearty mountain hike,' chuckled Roy. 'Just my cup of tea!'

'Now, where was I?' I said, suitably gratified. 'Ah, yes: . . . *reaching a plateau beyond mere professional pride, working as one body with two heads, licking and plunging in and around her, the noise of the three liquid orifices filled the huge room more deafeningly than the most sophisticated sound system.*'

Silence descended. To my left, Kenneth Rose withdrew a hand-woven mauve hankie and began to wipe the sweat from his brow.

'Frankly, I'm lorst,' proclaimed Leslie Rowse, somewhat pettishly. 'Will someone tell me what they're all up to? Pot-holing is it? Cleaning a drain, perchance? Hardly the stuff of anthologies, one would have thought.'

Sensing that I was losing their confidence, I skipped yet more pages, but, by now, there was, as Mr Bond might have put it in one of his more elegant moments(!), no turning back.

'Another of my favourite passages from this . . . experimental, yes, *experimental* work, is to be found a little further on' I announced, flipping like billy-oh through the pages in search of something seemly. 'Aha! Here we are!' I said, and began to read.

'*She took it out inch by inch – not believing that there could be yet more and more of it. It must be a trick, like those long strings of coloured kerchiefs conjurors kid children with; she felt the same wonder now as she handled it. It was like a cosh wrapped in plush pink velvet: ten inches easily.*'

'Delightful! Delightful!' exclaimed Sir Harold encouragingly. 'Rarely have I encountered such a felicitous description of the nefarious delights of the Christmas Cracker! Onwards, ever onwards, dear Wallace!'

I continued, '*Do you like to eat pussy?' she asked*'.

'Pardon me,' said Roy, 'but did you say "pussy"? I'm very sorry, but I have a natural fondness for animals, unfashionable though that may be. May I ask why any character brought up in the central tradition of European literature would enjoy eating a cat? A bit off, I would have thought.'

Happily Sir Harold sprang to my defence. 'Misprint, my dear Roy,' he chipped in. 'Must mean "purée" – "Do you like to eat purée?"Some people don't, y'know. Never liked pineapple m'self: most uncouth of fruits. Proceed!'

I continued with my reading. '*Have you ever – er,*' I hesitated for my eye had caught a glimpse of my impending doom. '*Have you ever – *'

'Have you ever WHAT? One two, one two, my dear, can't wait all day,' barked Leslie, his usual tetchy self.

I played for time. 'I really do feel I mustn't hog too much time with my recitation, and Kenneth reads so very beautifully,' I argued.

'HAVE YOU EVER WHAT?!!!' roared Leslie once more, and the others seemed to share his curiosity.

'Naughty, Wallace, naughty! No time for tenterhooks! Conclude the passage, *s'il vous plaît.*' It was Sir Harold, demonstrating his easy acquaintance with the French tongue. Alas, I had no option.

'*Have you ever fucked a donkey?*' I said.

Needless to say, I rushed shame-faced to my room, and it was early nights all round. In the morning, I was informed by a senior butler that my breakfast had been set at the end of the garden, some two hundred yards from the others. Sir Harold was very good about it, allowing me to leave by the earliest possible train, but he gave me no hint of any subsequent invitation. No doubt this was the effect on civilisation Miss Burchill intended when she set pen to paper. If that be the case, civilisation will not lightly forgive her.

NICOLAE AND ELENA CEAUSESCU

An explanation

*W*ith the deposition and execution of President and Mrs *Ceausescu at the tail-end of 1989 came many calls from those with little experience of international affairs for explanations as to why various British VIPs had once seemed so friendly with a couple who were now portrayed as ruthless monsters. In his first and only public statement on the matter, Arnold offered a wholly convincing and at times deeply moving explanation for all his actions.*

W.A.

It has been brought to my attention that among the colour snaps that have been released in the West of Nicolae and Elena Ceausescu entertaining friends and contacts to a leisure-time barbecue-cum-fondue party in the extensive grounds of their summer home, the reassuring face of one Wallace Arnold savouring a goodly haunch of honeyed venison can oft be spied beaming in the background. In the light of recent events, a handful of one's less travelled friends have seen fit to question my presence at such agreeable yet controversial (dread word!) gatherings. To set the matter straight for once and for all, I now intend to go to the by no means inconsiderable bother of recounting in some detail my dealings with Sir Nicolae and Lady Elena. If this means that I am accused of blowing my own wind-instrument in praise of my key role as an

*'Lady Elena came down to breakfast with the proud beast
already boned and skinned.'*

ambassador for East–West relations during those stark years, then so be it.

I first made the acquaintance of the 'so-and-so's', as I subversively termed them behind their backs, at a cocktail party hosted by Sir David and Lady Judith Steel in the garden of their lovely home at Ettrick Bridge. The cream of British society was there, including Mr Robert Maxwell, looking resplendent in Romanian national costume, and, from o'er the glens, HRH the Duke of Edinburgh, a friend of Sir Nicolae's from way back, and a keen barbecuer to boot. It was at this intimate gathering that Sir David took delight in presenting Sir Nicolae with an adorable pedigree hunting dog called Gladstone. Such was the gratitude of the Ceausescus that on the morning of the very next day, Lady Elena came down for breakfast with the proud beast already boned and skinned, its handsome fur lending her neckline a touch of much-needed glamour.

My edition of *The Wit and Wisdom of Nicolae Ceausescu* (Pergamon Press £2.95) sprang from this first meeting, as did the subsequent volume, *Freedom's Hero: The Authorised Biography of Nicolae Ceausescu by Wallace Arnold* (Pergamon Press £3.95). But at no time did I regard the Romanian leader with anything less than the deepest suspicion, and I consistently argued against his policies to his face on my extended visits to his holiday villa in '73, '75, '78 (twice), '80, '83, '86 and 87. Probably as a result of my outspoken criticisms of his régime, our relations cooled shortly after the mass rally against him in Bucharest, and I still steadfastly refuse to do so much as honour his grave with a wreath.

If the price of freedom is the odd nibble of a chipolata, I see nothing agin' it. Those who mutter darkly of compromise forget how the well-honed word in the ear over a sumptuous spread of sweetmeats can be more powerful and constructive than any amount of tanks and guns. Muddle-headed I may be, but I like to think that some of my tough advice to Sir Nicolae hit home. Indeed, I can say with some confidence that, after a candid exchange in '86, he had learnt to mix a perfectly acceptable sauce vinaigrette on my return in '87.

A CHRISTENING

Including a friendly correspondence

*T*he following timely piece was written by Arnold the
very week that Mr Black, proprietor of the Daily
Telegraph, had exchanged forceful and very public letters
with his former Managing Director, Mr White, who had left
his organisation for Mr Murdoch's employ. It had emerged
that Mr Black was the godfather to the child of Mr White.
With typical thoughtfulness, Arnold insisted on the publication of this piece in order to 'clear the air' between these two
former friends.

W.A.

It was upon being asked to be one of the godfathers to
Mr Andrew White's young daughter that one first
started counting the spoons. Nevertheless, one
accepted the post with nothing short of alacrity, knowing that at the christening ceremony one would be
rubbing shoulders with the very noblest and most
righteous in the realm, and that a share option on the
little mite could well turn up dividends in the not-too-
distant future.

When the time came, one's fellow godparents were
all that one might have hoped for. Along with Mr
Black and his wife Cilla, there were Mr Hughie Green,
Mr Thomas Pink and Mr John Browne. The service
went without a hitch, amicable business letters being
exchanged between hymns. After a lusty rendition of
'Tantum Ergo', Mr Black nudged me, placed a hastily

scribbled missive in my paws, and whispered, 'Pass it on.' This I did, and hence it came to reside in the immaculately manicured hands of Mr White. Availing myself of the opportunity to peruse said missive o'er his shoulder, I read the following:

'Dear White, I am writing this purely to safeguard your, alas, hideously tarnished reputation. This is a purely private letter which I do not intend to make public until a full three minutes have passed. I have long defended, to all your many enemies, the imagination you brought to bear upon the potentially onerous task of de-manning the company. Sometimes you would deliver the burdensome news of impending dismissal wearing an amusing hat, sometimes in the form of a limerick, but always with *joie de vivre*. I remember with great affection our close friendship, a friendship firm enough to withstand, I do most strongly believe, the deep suspicion in which you will continue to be held by all sane persons. Your sincerely, Black.'

At the closing refrain of 'Faith of Our Fathers', while we assembled godparents were bolstering our loins for the statutory renunciation of evil, I received another nudge, this time from Mr White. 'Pass it on,' he whispered, handing me a sheet of the finest duck–egg Basildon Bond.

'Dear Black,' it read, 'thank you very much for your ludicrously emotional, absurdly intemperate, wholly mischievous, possibly libellous and grossly inaccurate letter, for which I am most grateful. No one can deny your tremendous achievement in appointing me to manage your business, and I will continue to nod my head with all the vigour at my disposal at all those who are now saying that without me you will disappear down the plug-hole. Yours sincerely, White.'

As Il Papa – an old pen-friend and business colleague of White from way back – prepared to anoint the babe-in-arms, we all of us in the cathedral felt that reverent frisson of spirituality, a frisson born of a shared respect for tradition, for economic realism and for modern Conservative values. The babe, alas, squealed.

THE YOUNG
CONSERVATIVES

A well-earned salute to the cream of a generation!

A rnold has always had a tremendous amount of time for *young people, as his involvement in the Duke of Edinburgh Award Scheme continues to remind us. Here, he pays tribute to their enthusiasm, their natural ebullience and their welcome return to Conservative values.*

W.A

I humbly admit that they see me as something of an hero, and with every good reason. The Young Conservatives honoured your doughty(!) scribe by inviting him to address their PJGPH (Paul Johnson Group for Peace and Harmony) at their Torquay conference, and I was flattered by the warmth of my reception. I am an unashamed admirer of the young, and, I am glad to report, vice versa. I have always admired their tremendous energy and their terrific feeling for their fellow humans, so often mis–channelled into a crude belief in 'helping the under–privileged' (spare us *that!*). But I have come away from Torquay with a renewed sense of their patriotism, their charm and, perhaps above all, their *joie de vivre*.

I was met off the locomotive at Torquay by a Young Conservative committee member who took pains to wipe the previous night's vomit off his cuff before greeting me warmly by the hand. He then introduced me to a young executive, resplendent in an 'I Love Maggie' cap, who, replacing his 'member' (dread word!), proceeded to fill me in on fifteen first-class reasons for the liberalisation of the draconian Anti-Slave Trade laws. And so to the meeting hall, where an occasionally silent turn-out of between six and eight listened carefully as I waxed lyrical on the topic of 'A Future for Conservative Thought? Wallace Arnold and the Rise of the Tory Intellectual'.

The questions that followed were brief and admirably incisive. 'What are we going to do about the nignogs, then?' was the first, and a clarion call for the re-introduction of cock-fighting constituted the second. I found the third and final question a little hard to catch, so vigorous had grown the burping and subsequent 'letting off' of Madam Chairman, but I believe it was something to do with whether I was a Roundhead or a Cavalier. Hardly topical maybe, but I endeavoured to keep my reply light-hearted, and was delighted to draw the occasional titter. I then followed my hosts to the saloon bar, which they had entered some time earlier with a view to saving me a seat. Alas, they had failed in this respect, but I was quite happy to 'perch' on the arm of a chair occupied by an under-treasurer, who was catching up on some well-deserved sleep in a pool of cider sprinkled any-old-how with salt-and-vinegar potato 'crisps'.

The next day, I journeyed to the main hall to watch as the Prime Minister paid tribute to the Conservative youth of today. 'You are our Future!' she exclaimed, and my eyes scanned the hall, able, at a glance, to see beyond the temporary skin problems therein displayed and to pick out the Cecil Parkinsons and the David Waddingtons of tomorrow. As I left that hall, my heart swelling with pride, I thought to myself that the best of our youth are now forsaking the lure of Socialism, women, 'pop music', long hair and 'free love' to return to the more congenial pastures of modern Conservatism, and about time too.

MR TOM DRIBERG
(LORD BRADWELL!)

Luncheon with Thomas could be a mixed pleasure

A rnold's friendships in the world of politics are legion. Men and women from both sides of the House respect his judgement, his highly developed sense of the ridiculous and, perhaps above all, his discretion. He would occasionally partake of luncheon with the notorious Tom Driberg, whom he here recalls, but their acquaintance, he attests, never developed in any way whatsoever beyond enjoying a quick bite together. A moving vignette: *note the writer's strong sense of compassion.*

W.A.

It was while I was dining with Tom Driberg *à deux* at the Gay Hussar in – what was it? '64? '65? – that he first confessed to me that he fancied Willie Whitelaw something rotten. 'You'll get over it, Tom, you'll get over it,' I purred, sticking my fork into an Hungarian spicy sausage, but I now think that perhaps he never did.

There had been unrequited passions before Willie, of course – he once confided in me that he would sacrifice his country house, his parliamentary seat, his every-thing, for just one lick of the young Roy Hattersley's earlobe – but none, I think, meant as much.

While Victor served up some *dobas torte*, Tom leant over in my direction, grabbed hold of my lapels and in that urgent, well-educated voice asked me why Willie simply would not listen. 'Be a petal, Wallace,' he whispered. 'Tell him that I will die with the name

'Tom did everything to attract Willie, but to no avail.'

Willie writ large upon my heart. Tell him his Dribbles is waiting, waiting, waiting.'

I tried to distract him with talk of nationalisation of the steel industry, but he would have none of it. I knew then, as I know now, that Willie would be game to no locker-room tomfoolery, but looking around the restaurant at the other politicians therein assembled, I could espy no suitable alternative. 'What about Jim Callaghan?' I ventured. Jim was at that moment polishing off some sauerkraut. 'Jemima Callaghan?' replied Tom. 'Ugh! Next you'll be suggesting Georgina Brown!'

Tom did everything to attract Willie, but to no avail. At one point, he even hired a female grouse costume from Monty Berman's shop in Covent Garden, took chirruping lessons from a gifted ornithologist and spent many a wasted day hanging around the moors on the offchance of catching Willie's eye. 'He winked at me! He did! He winked at me!' he once told me, following a speech Willie had made in the Commons calling for a calmer, more considered approach to things, but I now think that he must have been imagining it.

Perhaps to distract himself from this hopeless infatuation, Tom threw himself headlong into numerous affairs. He once boasted to me that he had had his way with every member of the National Executive except Barbara Castle, all but one subdeacon on the General Synod of the Church of England, three-quarters of the cast of the Black and White Minstrels and the entire Health and Safety Executive of the TUC General Council, and all in the space of a single afternoon.

For the last 15 years of his life, Tom bombarded Willie with invitations to the ballet, invitations to the Christmas concerts of the Llanelli Male Voice Choir, and invitations to *thés dansants* at the Waldorf, always to find them swiftly returned with a typically courteous rebuff. Only once did Willie show any sign of consternation. 'You may address me as William or Willie,' he wrote back to Tom, refusing a particularly effusive invitation for a weekend for two in Casablanca, 'but I'm afraid I must absolutely draw the line at Wilhelmina.'

HRH THE DUKE OF EDINBURGH AND MR ANDY WARHOL

Though a keen water-colourist himself, Prince Philip draws the line (!) upon meeting Andy Warhol!

*R*eviewing a selection of books about the recently deceased *New York artist Andy Warhol for* Punch *magazine, Arnold recalls a fateful meeting between his close friend and confidant Prince Philip and the late artist. Note Arnold's extraordinary attention to detail, his masterful character sketches of both Prince and artist, and his sharp ear for dialogue.*

W.A.

To be utterly frank, he was not what one would describe as normal. Even in the golden age of *Punch*, when Mrs Libby Heiney was penning her marvellous comic *tour de force* ('Brief Encounters in the local Launderette!!') and that veritable Maestro of Mirth, Sheridan Morley, was, in his own delicious phrase, 'waxing lyrical' in a six-part series celebrating the Zany Vision of William Davis of that parish, Andy Warhol never took out a regular subscription.

On his first, and, I believe, only visit to the world-renowned *Punch* lunch – estimable repast – Mr Warhol cut an awkward figure. Coren had summoned yours truly to his office that morn. 'Wallace,' he had said, for he relished the opportunity to address all members of the staff by their Christian names. 'Wallace, I have decided that you should be seated next to Mr Andy Warhol at luncheon today. He is, as you may have gathered, an American – '

'No irony,' I chipped in.

'Come again?' quoth Coren.

'No irony,' I repeated. 'Our American cousins, for all their infectious optimism and straight talk, have no understanding of irony.'

'Quite,' quoth Coren, launching into an hilarious comic fantasy in which he took on the *persona* of a Chinaman asking for a packet of 'irony' at a delicatessen ('Me Wantee Ironee, Me Crackee Many Joke With It'). When he had finished his Dotty Discourse, Coren drew himself up, sighed a deep sigh, and said, 'I have chosen you to sit next to Mr Warhol because I myself have to sit beside His Royal Highness the Duke of Edinburgh, and Libby will be partnering our other distinguished visitor, the renowned broadcaster Mr Jimmy Young. We are very keen that they should all, as it were, "get on," so we have chosen you to "bridge the gap".'

At the time I was the justly distinguished Motoring Correspondent of *Punch*, famous among my fellow humorists for my 'light touch', a way I had of injecting merriment into even the most 'serious' of subjects with a few deft strokes of my pen. If Mr Warhol needed a little up-cheering, Coren obviously felt that I was the man to perform the feat.

His Royal Highness was the first to arrive. He was a great favourite among the *Punch* regulars, and we would roar heartily at his numerous 'quips', some of them of too outspoken a nature to reprint here, I fear! 'And may I be allowed to present to Your Majesty,' began Coren, turning to Yours Truly, 'Mr Wallace Arnold, our illustrious Motoring Correspondent these past seventeen years.'

'Cars . . . Cars . . . ' quipped His Royal Highness, the Duke of Edinburgh, with little more than a moment's hesitation. 'Four-wheeled vehicles for the driving thereof!!!!'

Of course, we all fell about. I then felt I should reply to this excellent jest, and so, quick as a flash, I returned the riposte. 'I hope Your Majesty will not think me impudent to attempt to "cap" his already quite splendid humorous aphorism pertaining to our four-wheeled friends,' I interjected. 'But may I add that, in selecting a car for use over any distance, one would be well advised to ensure that it was in full possession of a steering wheel – not to mention an engine!!!'

Needless to say, it went down a treat, and a right royal gale of laughter emerged from the mouth of the Duke, who is, might I also add, an interesting and thought-provoking man in his own right, and genuinely concerned, to boot. Jimmy Young, too, saw the joke, shooting me an encouraging wink.

At this point in the proceedings, just as the gong went for luncheon, in came Mr Andy Warhol, looking like goodness-knows-what. He brought with him a selection of rapscallions, con-men and ne'er-do-wells, all, I need hardly say, utterly uninvited, many, I suspect, 'high' on drugs of every shade and hue. The Duke's smile soon changed to something approaching a scowl, and I heard the words 'thorough-going pansy' splutter from his tensed lips. Arnold edged him away from the firing line of the Duke, attempting to engage him in a little civilised conversation.

'Do you know my good friend Basil Boothroyd?' I asked, striving to seek 'common ground'. 'I believe he once visited New York.'

'That's great,' replied Mr Warhol. 'Really great.'

'And Paul Johnson? You'd love to meet Paul Johnson! Doesn't mind what he says, old Paul!'

'That's great,' he replied once more. 'Really great.'

Steering him into the dining-room, seating the artist

(pardon my French!) and his entourage well away from the Duke, I continued to make the running.

'I'll tell you who you simply *must* look up while you're in town and that's Bill Deedes, tremendous character!'

'That's great,' said Warhol. 'Really great.'

And so our conversation continued all the way through luncheon. Come the port, Alan asked for our favourite humorous anecdotes concerning bus conductors. After many an amusing tale, it came to Mr Warhol's turn.

'That's great,' he said. 'Really great.'

By this time, the Duke was seething, and was led away, threatening to cancel the palace subscription forthwith. Needless to say, Mr Warhol was never again invited to break bread with Mr Punch.

Looking up the entry for that day in the voluminous *Andy Warhol Diaries*, I have experienced something akin to outrage. Under 'July 15th 1982', Warhol writes: 'Cabbed ($5.50) to lunch at *Punch* magazine. The guy next to me kept picking his nose. I guess he might have been gay because he kept telling me to look up all these British guys. He was *so* boring, no sense of irony or anything. But at least Prince Philip, who's married to the Queen of England and is probably quite rich, was there. He was really nice and seemed to be really interested in me. Cabbed back ($5.50).'

I feel that there is little point in going on with this review. I am proud to say that I have not deigned to open the other books, all by the assorted weirdos he dragged in with him. He was, as I have said, not normal. And let's leave it at that.

A FLEET STREET FRIENDSHIP

A tribute to Harry Smethwick

Towards the end of the 1980s, a tradition of waspishness began to grow in the obituary columns of newspapers and magazines, particularly when the deceased was a writer or journalist. In the spring of 1990, Mr George Gale wrote such a hard-hitting appreciation of Henry Fairlie, his great friend who had died the week before, that three members of Mr Fairlie's family wrote letters of complaint. But Wallace Arnold was never of that sniping ilk. When his own friend, Mr Harry Smethwick, died, just two weeks after Fairlie, Arnold wrote this sympathetic, touching but honest appraisal of the man.

W.A.

Harry Smethwick, the distinguished journalist who died last week, was commonly known by his friends simply as 'Niffy' Smethwick. He didn't wash much, if at all, and his breath was of such velocity as to clear the public bar, but we loved him all the more dearly for it.

In writing this warm-hearted tribute to a dear and trusted friend, I must begin by tracing the source of our acquaintance. Upon first meeting in the downstairs bar at the National Gallery, we immediately recognised each other as soul mates. I was the more intelligent, attractive and popular, but he knew more about grey-hounds, or so he claimed. Even then – and I am now talking about the late '50s, that remarkable era – he possessed the purple face and idiosyncratic gait (saving on shoe-leather, he chose to hop everywhere) that endeared him to all those who tolerated him.

His taste in women was patchy. Often, when we were arguing long and noisily over our cream stouts in the upstairs bar of the Sir John Soane Museum, a discarded woman would arrive at our table, placing a naked breast somewhat disconcertingly into his pint pot so as to place a barrier between him and his beloved beverage. On other occasions, while we were putting the world to rights in the saloon bar of the Imperial War Museum, a fiancée or other would appear, decked out in full wedding garb, pages and bridesmaids trailing, demanding to know why he was not at the altar.

He would treat his women appallingly, often forcing them to give him piggyback rides to work rather than succumbing to the more expensive option of catching the tube. But they loved him for it, and, in turn, were invited to join him on the office floor, where he would entertain them with his passionately held views on Archbishop Makarios or the rise of skiffle.

But it would be wrong to give the impression that Niffy was a plaster saint. If he had any faults, they were many and varied. He had a mulish streak, delivering a swift kick to anyone who stood immediately behind him, and going 'Eeyore! Eeyore!' whenever the subject of food cropped up in conversation. By the late '60s, his purplish hue had become tinged with green, so that he would oft find himself perused in the lounge bar of the British Museum by passers-by who had inadvertently mistaken him for a wall-map of the Western Isles.

He delighted, of course, in my friendship, as I in turn grew to tolerate his. I offered him social standing, a keen intellect, political *savoir faire* and the easy charm of the well-bred, while he would from time to time offer me a slim panatella. Many were his qualities. He was always courteous, except when rude. He was quite good at cooking broccoli. He could tell a joke, though not well. He was rarely slow to join us in laughing at himself, and, if the need arose, could be swiftly laid out with a swift jab to the chin. Through it all, he was sustained by his friends, or friend. He was a difficult man, but he loved me dearly.

FORSOOTH

An etymological exploration

*Arnold has long seen himself primarily as a wordsmith,
and, as such, he takes an almost obsessive interest in the
history of words. This fascination can be witnessed throughout his writings, but most particularly in his appreciative
essay on the* Oxford English Dictionary *(see page 114)
and in this piece, later widely reprinted throughout the world.*

W.A.

That estimable wordsmith, the blessed Philip Howard,
has produced another wholly agreeable tome on the
toing and froing of that most delicate of instruments,
the English language. The opening chapters of *Winged
Words*, for such is its title, deal with many of the more
wince-making uses for decent, old, house-trained
words, for instance the employment of 'hopfully' to
mean 'energetic running using only one leg'. But the
larger part of the *oeuvre* is given over to an wholly
engrossing investigation into that most charming of
English words, 'forsooth'. It is, opines the blessed
Philip, in for something of a revival, and a jolly good
thing too.

Only last Sunday, Terry Worsthorne planted an
unabashed 'forsooth' bang in the middle of his leading
article, and it was fascinating to watch it take flower.
Terry's provocative but entirely convincing essay
argued with unassailable logic that the lurid tendency,
pioneered in the Sixties, for *Guardian*-reading couples

to 'kiss' – a practice wherein one 'partner' places his lips upon those of another 'partner', culminating in an effect too horrid to describe – is to be blamed for the rampant child abuse now sweeping the country. Terry put the blame fairly and squarely on Mr Kenneth Tynan, for was it not he who first intoned that ghastly word that rhymes with 'tuck' whilst appearing on the dread gogglebox? But it was Terry's telling use of 'forsooth' that clinched the argument. Justice Butler-Sloss had argued with feminine logic (contradiction in terms?!) for more social workers. This demand was smartly refuted by Terry with the single, devastating sentence, 'More social workers forsooth.' Game, set and match to Mr Worsthorne.

Thus to the 'forsooth' half of *Winged Words*. In the 18th century, it emerges, 'forsooth' was not a word in the strictest sense at all, but a not uncommon Christian name for a girl, as Terry's great, great, great, aunt, Miss Forsooth Worsthorne, knew to her cost.

But by the 1790s, it had become an indelible part of the language, meaning, literally, 'the user of this word is a sophisticated wit and iconoclast of the first order'. This meaning accounted for its great popularity in the first half of the 19th century, but it was, alas, frequently misused, so much so that by 1890 it was employed rarely and then only for its subsidiary meaning of 'spoon designed especially for the gathering of single strawberries'. Thus 'Could you please pass me the forsooth,' Mr Josiah Worsthorne, the noted bon viveur, was reported to have said, as late as 1910.

In our own day, a 'forsooth' is most widely used to mean a leather thong, exclusive to the homosexual community, though Terry's gratuitous reference to such a vile instrument in a family Sunday newspaper seems quite beyond my ken, and symptomatic of the malaise that began at some time during the 1960s.

MR LUCIAN FREUD

Even modern art needs its patrons!

*A*s Mr Jocelyn Stevens's guru at the Royal College of Art and a distinguished collector in his own right, Wallace Arnold is one of our leading patrons of modern art. Here, during the course of a lengthy and highly perceptive review of Works on Paper *by Lucian Freud, he lovingly recalls a dinner party at which his own sacrifices for art were seen to be second to none.*

W.A.

It was while we were all of us enjoying the melodious sound of Lord Goodman playing upon the lute towards the end of one of Bubbles Rothermere's artistic *soirées*, that the conversation turned towards the painting of one's portrait. All the leading *patrons de l'art moderne* were there, including Maurice Saatchi, David Sainsbury, Grey Gary, Lord Stevas and, of course, the irrepressible Bubbles herself, so one instinctively knew that one's 'grey cells' would acquire some pretty valuable knowledge.

'Henry Moore has done me,' triumphed Bubbles, the metalwork on her bikini-top glistening in the soft light of the chandelier.

'Excellent! Excellent!' chimed in Norman St John Stevas, who had been allowed in for a few mins to help out with the washing-up. 'And where can one see the finished product? Do tell!'

'Outside the new Droitwich Telephone Exchange.

It's a sculpture called "Bubbles". Very modern, of course,' explained our hostess. 'It consists of a vast boulder with a little stone on top. And the little stone has a great big hole in it.'

'Frankly, I can't get on with representational art,' protested Maurice Saatchi. 'Unlike you, Bubbles, I have always favoured the abstract. I am proud to say that I managed to get the late Jackson Pollock to do me. It's a close up of my face as a series of spots. Brilliant, quite brilliant.'

We all turned to Grey Gary, his face, too, seeming uncannily as if it had been run up by the late Mr Pollock in one of his moodier phases. 'My dear Grey,' said I, 'pray tell us the artist whom you have sponsored to portray your inner soul for eternity's delight!'

'Bacon,' said Grey.

'But we've just finished puds,' protested Bubbles.

'Francis Bacon,' repeated Grey. 'Stunning. It's a triptych entitled "Corpse on Slab". The first section portrays my kidneys, the second my left leg, severed and riddled with gangrene, and the third shows my whole body, cut into eight separate pieces with a cleaver. It was expensive, but well worth it.'

We all eyed him with no little envy. At last, Norman St John Stevas took a judicious breath and told us of his own portraitist. 'I swear by Bratby,' he declared. 'Full of colour, and such boldness and bravura! I'll always remember the session. I went along to his studio, paid over my £10,000, and then he asked me to remove my suit. This I did – with some reluctance, mind! – and he then told me to remove my socks and knickers too. "You're the artist," I said, and as I stood there completely starkers he proceeded to roll me in three different types of sticky paint – red, yellow and blue. I must say, he did have the decency to ask me to remove my spectacles before smearing the pot of green all over my face, and it all washed out of my hair quite easily after three or four weeks. Anyway, after he had rolled me all over in paint, he asked me to lie face up on the ground, and he then placed a blank canvas on top of me and walked over me again and again for close on half an hour, thus creating the most superb portrait for posterity. It's called "Rich Geezer Smeared with Colours", and I have recently lent it to the Museum of Contemporary Art in Toronto for their travelling exhibition, "Capitalist Bastards of the 20th Century".'

'Splendid,' said David Sainsbury. 'And it goes to prove what I have always said: that it is the business of the industrialist to lend support, where e'er he can, to the toiling artist.' He then played what one might describe as his 'trump card'. 'I myself,' he continued, 'have had the honour to purchase my portrait from many of the greatest geniuses of our day. Diane Arbus's stunning "Man with Sock over his Head in Central Park" is of course, of me, and so is Christo's stunning piece of conceptual art, "Industrialist Wrapped in Polythene Suspended from Sydney Harbour Bridge on a Damp Morning". And I need hardly tell you that I was the inspiration, both financial and aesthetic, behind Gilbert and George's flamboyant masterpiece, "Nitwit With More Money Than Sense Seen From Six Different Angles for a Vast Sum of Readies", and so I have earned, I like to think, my little place in the History of Modern Art, pshaw!'

'All this talk of art has made me come over all hungry!' laughed Bubbles, placing a leg of lamb in her mouth, her little finger daintily outstretched, hastily supplementing her new snack with a small jar of mint sauce tossed neatly down her throat.

Lord Goodman's lute piped the final notes of its plaintive tune, and its player looked up, his eyes positively abrim with pride. 'You're none of you as committed to the ideals of modern art as I am!' he proclaimed, a touch aggressively, 'Bacon! Gilbert and George! Arbus!

Bratby! Prettifiers one and all! They merely bow and scrape to the vanity of the rich! I have been painted by a REAL ARTIST. I have been painted by no less an artist than Lucian Freud. He might cost that bit more, but he sure makes you ugly for your money. Look! Here I am!'

So saying, he reached for his briefcase to withdraw the book that I am now privileged to review. 'Howzat!' he said, turning to page 90. 'Now that's what I call Art!'

We all gazed in envy at the hideous representation we saw before us. Entitled 'Lord Goodman in his Yellow Pyjamas, 1987', it resembled nothing so much as a manic depressive wart-hog that had recently resorted to the meths bottle. It was, said the small type, one of an edition of fifty. 'I sent the other 49 out to my more influential clients as Christmas cards,' said Goodman. 'They were most impressed. Business is booming.'

'Oooh! All this talk of business is bad for the waistline,' chirruped Bubbles. 'Black Forest Gâteau, anyone?'

By now, it might have struck the reader, as it was beginning to strike my hostess and fellow guests, that it was about time one Wallace Arnold chipped in with his twopenn'orth. Surely dear Wallace was not guilty of neglecting the Arts? I could feel the question quivering on the lips of all present. Maurice Saatchi started eyeing me strangely, as if I might be one of those dread philistines against whom Sir Harold Acton has so sagely warned us. I waited until the tension had stretched to snapping point before I launched in.

'I too have been the subject of a painting by Mr Lucian Freud,' I announced, pointing to the book. 'And, what is more, it too is displayed therein!'

Lord Goodman looked most put out and flick-flick-flicked through the pages with a rapidity that belied the girth of his forefinger. 'I can't find you anywhere,

Wallace,' he said, triumphantly, sweat pouring from his brow.

'Please turn to page 7,' I declared forthwith. The entire gang had now gathered around the ample form of Goodman, their beady eyes glued to the tortured tome.

'Sorry, old chap,' said Lord Goodman, once he had located the page in question, 'you're not here at all. Page seven just has a close-up of Lucian's stark and broody masterpiece, "Man's Penis with Thistle Attached". I'm afraid you don't get a look in, dear boy.'

'It's mine,' I said, my eyes glistening with pride. 'The minute Lucian saw me, he said, "Off with those clothes" and then he stuck a large thistle to my John Thomas. The wounds are still with me. Not bad for £20,000. One for the boardroom, eh, Goodman?'

Goodman was visibly peeved, Maurice looked daggers, Grey Gary started stamping his foot, a tear of jealousy ran down the cheeks of poor Norman, and David Sainsbury let out a muffled groan. Wallace Arnold had once again established his credentials as Britain's foremost art lover.

'But you simply MUST stay for Blancmange,' whimpered Bubbles, as the five of 'em trooped dejectedly into the cold, cold night.

'I might manage just *un petit peu*,' I said, retucking my napkin.

MR GRAHAM GREENE

Shadowy figure in a twilight world

Few have penetrated the almost obsessive secrecy of novelist Graham Greene with such precision and understanding as his friend and confidant, Wallace Arnold. In this seminal piece, reprinted here for the first time, Arnold describes the extraordinary private world of one of our greatest novelists.

W.A.

We are all by now familiar with the well-worn features of my notoriously private friend Mr Graham Greene, that profoundly anonymous man who, in a desperate bid for the obscurity he so craves, has taken to restricting his exclusive interviews to no more than two a week. In recent years, Graham has gone to great lengths to disguise his identity on his visits to London, now donning black leathers and tin helmet to parade as just another motorcycle messenger round the literary salons of Bedford Square, now dressing as Santa when taking cocktails at Le Caprice. Alas, I regret to say that, in my experience, the placard he wears throughout his annual sojourn at the Ritz ('I AM NOT GRAHAM GREENE') often fails to deter the eagle-eyed.

We go back yonks, Graham and I. Many argue that I am the original for Mr Sheen in the flawed masterpiece *The Hell of Unreason* (later filmed as *The Love Bug*), and that I share the intense, often tortured Catholicism of Mr Mann in *Journey to Death* (later filmed as *Bedknobs and Broomsticks* with David Tomlinson) but I recognise myself more fully as the questing intellectual Emilio Grotti in *The Miserable and Even More Miserable* (later filmed as *Funny Old World* with Norman Wisdom).

I remember to this day lunching with Graham at Rules in '59. Worried lest he be recognised, he had arrived disguised as a fish-finger, only to be served by an unwitting waiter to an impatient diner. As luck would have it, the aforesaid diner recognised his fish-finger to be a novelist of international repute, but only in the nick of time. Once again, Greene had cheated fate. 'How did you guess that I was not a fish-finger?' asked the ever-inquisitive Graham. 'You forgot to breadcrumb your nose,' replied the diner. The incident formed the basis of *The Confidential Fish-Finger*, later published as *The Confidential Agent* after extensive re-working.

Greene's friendships, though few, have been extraordinarily close. I well remember dropping in on his Antibes basement one evening to be greeted by Fidel Castro bearing a tray of 'Hula Hoops', quite excellent cheese savouries, and there in a corner was Kim Philby, tucking into a generous plateful of Alphabetti Spaghetti with none other than the late Maurice Chevalier. Greene himself, fearful of being recognised, was dressed as a deck-quoit.

His biographer, Professor Sherry, though thorough, has missed the occasional public appearance, including Graham's guest slot on *Juke Box Jury* (1965), his Morecambe and Wise Christmas Special (1973) and, more recently, his cameo role in '*It Ain't 'Alf 'ot, Mum*' (1979) in which he played the role of the pansy croupier for just five episodes. Personally, I consider the self-effacing charm he brought to his job as anchorman of BBC/TV's *Come Dancing* (1974–5) to have been consistently underrated, and I trust that the good Professor gives it his fullest attention in the forthcoming second volume.

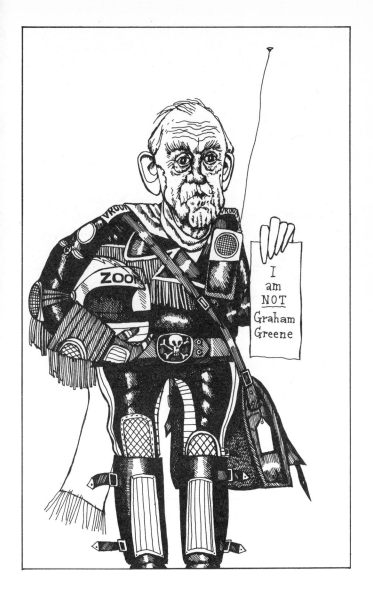

'In recent years, Graham has gone to great lengths to disguise his identity.'

A GREENER BRITAIN

Conservatives really do car!

*S**uch is Arnold's skill at the light-hearted essay that many commentators have neglected his more reflective and considered side. Here he modestly reveals the part he played in the renaissance of the great city of Liverpool, whilst simultaneously reviewing a book titled* Green Parenting. *This is likely to become one of the key texts to understanding the green movement in Britain during the 1980s.*

W.A.

As far back as the Seventies (dread decade!) I was the treasurer of a go-ahead group known as the Caring Conservatives. Sick to the back teeth with the union-dominated excesses of British Rail, we were a small gang of like-minded folk who had pledged ourselves to driving our own vehicles to the capital, hence the term 'Car-ing Conservatives'.

Owing to the liquidities of the English tongue, the Caring Conservatives grew to have an immense influence within the Party, and my position as a senior committee member did my reputation no harm at all. A decade on, after the riots in Liverpool, I was to receive a call from Mr Michael Heseltine, speaking on his car-phone.

'Wallace!' he exclaimed. 'Do you care as I care?'

'Care?' I replied. 'Care? Care? Oh, care?' It was a word I had not heard for yonks.

'Well,' he said. 'Do you? Do you?'

'Rather!' I enthused. When a top Tory talks about care, one knows that there will be well-remunerated committee work involved.

'Then join me, Wallace, join me!' Through the phone, I heard the distinctive sound of the theme tune to the Gloria Hunniford Radio Two programme striking up. 'I'll ring you right back,' said Michael, who has long had something of a 'pash' on Gloria, sharing the same hairdresser and so on.

Ringing back during the very first news–break, Michael made clear his demands. 'I have been set the task of breathing new life into Liverpool,' he said, 'and I want you, Wallace, to be my lungs.'

Before I knew it, I found myself on an all-party fact-finding mission to Liverpool in the company of four distinguished celebrity advisers, Michael at the helm. Each of us had been hand-picked for the particular talents we could bring to bear on the great city of Liverpool: Bubbles, Lady Rothermere, for her skills at making the world a happier place, Johnny Mortimer, for his very real understanding of how ordinary people live, Sir Roymond Strong, for his marvellous way with flower arrangements, Lady Antonia Fraser, for her passionate commitment to bettering the lot of the working man, and myself, Wallace Arnold, for my masterly use of the language and my undoubted flair for public relations.

By way of kicking off, Michael treated us to something of a pep-talk, his hair bobbing and billowing in the fine, manly wind provided by the Liverpool docks. 'Each of you has been alloted a pad and a pen,' he trumpeted. 'And upon our return from this morning's fact-finding mission, I want to see those pads full to the brim with Inner City Initiatives!'

Setting off in our open-topped double-decker, we all dutifully started to jot down our ideas for initiatives, though dear Bubbles had some trouble with her pen at the outset. 'It's so long since I've used one of these,' she complained. 'Remind me: which end does one use?'

After a singularly gruelling quarter of an hour, we returned to base, our fact-finding now over. The time had come for tough talking and hard choices, difficult decisions that would determine at a stroke the future lives of the citizens of this once great city.

Outside the Committee Room at the Adelphi Hotel, photographers from the World's Press were clamouring for snapshots of six such distinguished visitors. 'Such a nuisance,' said Michael, his personal stylist patting his legs with a pleasantly aromatic yet discreet and very masculine after-shave, 'but I suppose we must go along with them.'

Alas, the picture-snappers seemed keen for us to pose meeting the ordinary (dread understatement!) men and women of Liverpool. 'I honestly think that one can take these things too far,' I protested, but Michael complied with their request. 'Where can one get a handful of ordinary Liverpudlians, do you think?' he asked a highly-skilled government boffin.

'Liverpool?' suggested the boffin.

'Hmmm,' said Michael. 'You could try it, I suppose.'

Within minutes, a small posse of bobbies has mustered some ordinary people of Liverpool who were willing to pose, for an undisclosed fee, with Mr Michael Heseltine MP and the distinguished members of his fact-finding mission. 'Look as if you're ascertaining their views,' whispered Michael, as we held out our hands for them to shake. 'Views?' said Bubbles, Lady Rothermere. 'No one loves views more than I. And sunsets I simply *adore*. But frankly, I don't hold out much hope for any views *here*, darling. Looks *perfectly ghastly* to me.'

Our hobnobbing with the ordinary people now thankfully at a close, we allowed our hands a brisk scrub before setting our caps to the problems facing

Liverpool. And so, in a delightfully (and characteristically) roundabout way, we come to the book presently under review. You see, the so-called 'Green' movement is nothing new. Far from it, forsooth. Most of the solutions proposed in Miss (Ms?!!) Solomon's earnest tome first saw the light of day in that Adelphi Committee Room way back in '83. Sir Roymond Strong, called up to speak first, proposed 'gorgeous bunches of flowers – and let's not spare the fuchsias! – to be positioned in exquisite vases hither and thither throughout the slummy-wummies,' whilst Lady Antonia Fraser made an impassioned plea for some decent taramasolata.

Bubbles, Lady Rothermere brought the 'Green' issue smack bang in the forefront by stressing the need for grassy spaces. 'Why not knock down all those ghastly smelly houses and pay the little people in them to push off and then you could have a seriously nice park,' she suggested. Johnny Mortimer, on the other hand, emphasised the dietary aspects of a 'Green' revolution in Liverpool. 'Good Lord,' he uttered in that marvellously *civilised* voice of his. 'One saw startlingly little evidence of even a halfway-decent *bistro* in Toxteth. Open up a few first-class but inexpensive *brasseries* in the area – veg soup followed by an authentic cassoulet, plus, say, *creme brûlée* for afters, a little Vivaldi in the background, perhaps readings from *Rumpole* every Thursday night (do forgive that small *plugette*, Michael!) – and I can't see anyone in their right mind wanting to riot, or at any rate not until after the decaf *cappuccino* has materialised.'

I myself made a variety of prophetic 'Green' proposals – a ban on all whale-fishing on the Mersey, no shooting of butterflies between the hours of six and eight, hats to be worn during Ozone Layer open hours – which are nowadays commonplace. Shame on you then, Miss Solomon, for the wilful and pernicious exclusion – between 'alternative medicine' and 'authority, acceptance of' in your index – of the pioneering, gloriously green name of 'Arnold, Wallace'.

THE FAMILY GREER

*Genealogy can be fascinating – but, Arnolds
apart, it is rarely wise to dig too deep!*

*This fascinating disquisition on ancestry, albeit Austra-
lian, was occasioned by the publication of the tome,*
Daddy, I Hardly Knew You, *an investigation into her
father's life by former Sixties hothead Germaine Greer. In the
course of her searches, Germaine had discovered that her
father's real name was not Greer but Greeney – an alteration,
the better born might be forgiven for thinking, that was
scarcely worth the bother!*

W.A.

Every family has its quirks. I believe that, as recently as
the 17th century, one of my less illustrious ancestors
chose to call himself Wallace Arnald (*sic*) in a bid to 'lose
himself' in the crowd. My review copy of Miss (Ms!)
Germaine Greer's new tome informs me that the bonny
lass's papa suffered from something of the same 'identity crisis', as the balding boffins term it. Small world,
though: imagine my astonishment at discovering that
Greer senior was none other than Reg Greeney, a pal of
mine from way back.

Unstable character, to be sure. I first knew him as
Reg Greedy, 'The Gourmand from Google Creek', as
he was then, one of the rich cast of characters immorta-
lised in my classic travelogue, *Arnold in the Outback*.
Oddly enough, when next I bumped into him he
introduced himself as Reg Grumbly. 'Rum old world',
he kept repeating, his eagle-eye searching for the smal-
lest cloud in a honey-blue sky.

A gap of some years passed before I was to encounter him again. I was partaking of a modest yet agreeable luncheon at the Garrick when I perchanced to recognise a stranger exchanging repartee with a small group including Terry Worsthorne, Jimmy Tarbuck and Bruce Forsyth. 'I say,' I said. 'Aren't you Reg Grumbly, né Greedy?' Looking me firmly in the eye, he told me no, his name was now Reg Graspy, and could I see my way to lending him a fiver? 'Nice to see you,' quipped Brucie, 'to see you, nice,' and the group, which included, if memory serves, Sir Robin Day and the late Arthur Askey, roared with uninhibited laughter.

By 1981, my fast-moving career had taken me close to the heart of Conservative Central Office, and it was there, while swapping light-hearted banter with Sir Alfred Sherman in a corridor, that I received a familiar tap-tap on the shoulder. 'Wallace!' came the sound of an all-too-familiar voice. 'Remember me? Reg Greeky? Fancy a kebab?' Sure enough, wearing the full dress regalia of the *Evzones*, Reg had managed to take control of a major government Think-Tank, and, I am now led to believe, was a mere whisker away from persuading the Prime Minister that the National Brew should henceforth be retsina.

His restless personality saw no end to his name-changes. As Reg Greasy, he made great headway in the National Trust, while as plain Greavsie he became a television celebrity well-loved by many millions. But it was as Reg Gravy that I prefer to remember him, a gentleman from excellent stock. We are none of us entirely sure of our own identity; even my best friends tell me that there is something infinitely enigmatic about my own prismatic personality, as my forthcoming autobiography, *Wallace, We'd Like To Know You Better*, makes absolutely clear.

MR MICHAEL HESELTINE

The Blue Peter years

*A*rnold has long been convinced that knowledge of a man's *formative years can do much to illuminate the course of his subsequent career. This rare insight into the early years of Michael Heseltine did much to alert the Conservative Party and its supporters to the potential threat it faced from a man who was so loudly proclaiming his loyalty to their leader, and is remembered as one of Arnold's most timely and influential pieces.*

W.A.

It must have been 1962 – or was it 1963? – that, invited to appear on the popular new children's television programme *Blue Peter* in order to launch their Personal Hygiene Christmas Appeal, I first encountered the then junior presenter of the show, Michael Heseltine.

Clad in off-white oiled arran polo-neck, wearing a sou'wester and wellington boots two sizes too large, the young Michael made a winning companion to the young. One week, he would be bob-sleighing in Switzerland and the next he would be playing the pantomime dame in an hilarious seasonal studio recreation, but even at our first meeting I could tell straightaway that here was a young man who wanted, to employ the parlance of the time, 'to go places – and fast'.

'I fully support the lead and direction given to this programme over a number of years by Miss Valerie Singleton,' he announced just after the programme in

*'I could tell straight away that here was a young man who
wanted, to employ the parlance of the time,
"to go places" – and fast.'*

question went on air, 'and I have no wish to challenge her for her position as senior presenter of *Blue Peter* either now or in the near future. I hope I make myself perfectly clear.' This was not scripted, of course – as far as one can remember, he had been pencilled in to introduce an item on making a simple farmyard scene out of sundry items of fuzzy-felt – but it did make one a mite apprehensive as to his real intentions. Certainly, Miss Singleton's hands betrayed a certain shakiness when, a little later in the programme, she came to construct a life-size model of an owl entirely from old packets of a leading brand of breakfast cereal.

Six months later, I found myself on the programme once more, presenting the aforesaid *Blue Peter* Award for Personal Hygiene to a well-scrubbed nine-year-old named Master Colin Moynihan (the very same! small world!) whose fingernails and backs-of-ears were, and, I am happy to say, still are, quite impeccable. Once again, Mike Tine, as he was then known, kicked off the show by pledging loyalty to the second presenter, Mr Christopher Trace, defying any young viewer to mention one single instance when he had failed to give Trace his full and unequivocal support. I must admit to being not wholly surprised when, a few weeks later, leafing through my *Telegraph*, I came across a news item to the effect that Mike was now happily taking up the reins as second presenter. Christopher then disappeared without, as the saying goes, trace(!).

Valerie must surely have breathed a sigh of relief when Michael took time off from an agreeable item on the History of Morris Dancing to announce his departure from the programme in order to pursue publishing interests. He concluded by stating firmly and absolutely that he had no intention of tripping up a single Morris Dancer either then or during their performance. I daresay some were taken aback five minutes later, during the course of an enchanting 'Jig Through the Everglades', when a stealthily placed stick poked its way out of a backdrop to overturn the entire front rank of Morris Men. But not I, oh no, not I.

HIGH TABLE, HIGH CHAIRS

Little more than a list!

*A*rnold's memory for names has been justly praised in
many quarters, and it has been rarely shown to better
advantage than in this, a wide-ranging reminiscence of one of
the great Spectator *luncheon parties of the 1960s.*

W.A.

I wonder if anyone other than I managed to get all the
way through the farewell article written by our dear
departed editor in the *Sunday Telegraph* the other week?
He entertained his reader(s) with an agreeable saunter
through some of the highlights of his brief stint at the
steering wheel, including by no means uninteresting
anecdotes concerning some of the more colourful characters who have supped at the celebrated *Spectator* high
table o'er the years.

Might I add one or two of my own reminiscences
from my somewhat longer association with the journal? Well do I remember sitting in a celebrated *Spectator*
high chair in the March of 1968. My fellow guests were
Mr Enoch Powell, the leading politician and academic;
Miss Sandie Shaw, the *chanteuse*, whose magnificent
efforts with 'Puppet on a String' had gained Britain first
place in the Eurovision Song Contest of that year; the
Ayatollah Khomeini, at that time an up-and-coming

humorous essayist and co-presenter with Miss Muriel
Young of BBC TV's *Six O'Clock Club*, whose waspish
tongue and severity of judgement was even at that early
stage earning him something of a name for himself; the
Duke and Duchess of Windsor, fresh from a successful
season at the De La Warr pavilion, Bexhill-on-Sea; Mr
Somerset Maugham; the Kray Brothers, taking a well-
earned break from rehearsals for that week's *What's my
Line?*, hosted by the irascible Gilbert Harding; and
George Weidenfeld, or Gorge Widenfed as he then was,
owing to a proof-reader's error.

Others who gathered to partake of the assorted
sweetmeats at that memorable luncheon included Mr
Reg Varney, later to achieve an international reputation
for his leading role in *On the Buses*; Emperor and Mrs
Hirohito, over here on a flying visit to catch Dame
Anna Neagle in *Carousel*; Mr 'Teasy-Weasy' Raymond,
then famous as the initiator of the celebrated 'Peregrine
Worsthorne' humorous column in the *Sunday Telegraph*, later to become better known as a world-class
hairdresser; four members of the now defunct 'Black
and White Minstrels' team, including a fully blacked-
up Mr Kenneth Rose, later to gain prominence as a
diarist and biographer but then concentrating his ener-
gies on light-hearted renditions of the early hits of Al
Jolson; Professor Hugh Trevor-Roper, who had
arrived as a Tinned Peach in Heavy Syrup, having been
misinformed that it was one of those Come-as-a-Fruit
luncheon parties that were then enjoying something of
a vogue; Mr and Mrs Bamber Gascoigne and the two
competing teams from an early edition of *University
Challenge*, plus jocular mascots; and last but by no
means least our then proprietor, the Scandinavian band
leader Mr James Last, accompanied by leading
members of his rhythm section. Oddly enough, with
such an illustrious guest-list, it now seems extraordi-

nary that I am unable to remember a thing that happened before, during or after that luncheon, though we might well have had a rather good brie, and perhaps a stick or two of celery.

THE INDEPENDENT

Behind the scenes at a superb operation!

A rnold leafs thróugh a tome celebrating the launch of the Independent, adding his own inimitable aperçus *along the way. Note his skilled use of the telling anecdote.*

W.A.

I see that the amusing – but occasionally waspish! – cartoonist Mr Nicholas Garland has 'spilt the beans' on his fellow staff at that most admirable of publications, the *Independent*. Though I have yet to peruse his estimable publication, I am reliably informed that some of his 'in-house' (dread words!) revelations are extraordinary. 'May I borrow a paper-clip, old boy?' their distinguished columnist Sir William Rees Moog asks their distinguished editor, Miss (Ms!) Andrea Whittam-Smith, and the reply comes – quick as the proverbial flash – 'By all means, William . . . Take two'!!! Future anthologists of contemporary anecdotalia will be leaping on said tome like ducks to H_2O, I would venture to hazard.

But on a deeper level, the book is not simply a rich fund of hilarious 'quips' and aphorisms from some of the most responsible scribes in Fleet Street. It shows how a mature and distinguished journal is put together, examining the pioneering spirit of the men (and women!) who managed to sink their differences to produce this most agreeable and least frivolous of products.

For the first time we are taken into the morning

conference, therein to witness the editorial policy of the newspaper at election time as it bounces back and forth in the most sophisticated manner. 'What about Labour?' says one leading political sage. 'Nah!' replies Rees-Moog himself. 'I fancy Conservative.' Ever the diplomatist, Ms Whittam-Smith intervenes: 'Any takers for Alliance?' A few hands go up. 'Well,' declares Andrea, 'I think it's only fair to advise our readers to sleep on it, and to make up their own minds, if poss, come the morning, if they would be so very kind.'

At another conference, the editor grows worried that the newspaper might betray too little sense of humour. 'Sense of *what*?' asks distinguished columnist Mr Peter Jenkins. 'Sense of humour,' replies Andrea. 'You know, now what do you call them? Jokes. That's it, jokes.' 'Spelt?' asks Jenkins. 'J-O-K-E-S,' replies Andrea, 'but the 'J' may well be silent. Origin possibly Swedish.' Nodding cautiously, conference decides to increase the daily input of okes to three, or four if there's an extra supplement on Saturdays.

One of the most striking aspects of Garland's moving tribute lies in its depiction of the honour that exists within this unique – and distinguished – institution. Without the traditional back-stabbing of Fleet Street, the staff were able to forge professional friendships, occasionally resulting in full intercourse, but with no obligation so to do. Though some of their banter might sound a touch acerbic to the outsider – I am thinking now of the occasion upon which Mr Ronald Kray, their Chief Sale-room Correspondent, threatens eight of the senior editorial staff with a sawn-off shotgun after the last paragraph of his excellent piece on 'The Soaring Price of *Sèvres*' has been 'trimmed ' – this must be seen in the broader context of a serious newspaper, whose award-winning slogan 'Dull We Are Not' still holds true to this day.

MRS ISHERWOOD

*Christopher and Valerie share a lilo – and end
up in the Divorce Court*

*R*eviewing *Val Hennessy's* A Little Light Friction,
*Arnold finds himself harking back to his own, highly
personal memories of Wystan, Harold, Christopher – and the
first Mrs Isherwood. It should be noted that Wystan Auden
and Wallace Arnold share the same initials.*

W.A.

Little is known of Val Hennessy in what one might call
literary (dread word!) circles, other than that, for a
short time in the late Sixties (loathsome decade!), she
was married to Christopher Isherwood. What quirk of
fate, one now wonders, was it that brought them
together? Isherwood seemed strangely attracted by her
penchant for plain speaking: she had described T.S.
Eliot's 'The Wasteland' as 'a handjob by a pain-in-the-
arse' in a lengthy article for Connolly's *Horizon*. She, in
turn, had simply adored the film of *Cabaret*, though she
found the book 'a bit wordy'.

It was not long, alas, before the two of them came to
blows. Closeted in Issyvoo's Californian retreat, Hennessy yearned for something more. They fell out over
literary matters ('If you are a camera,' screamed Hennessy, throwing a first edition of *Goodbye to Berlin* at its
author, 'then I'm a bloody bidet!') but also over friends.
Auden, for instance, had never hit it off with Hennessy's soul-mate and confidante Claire Rayner, and
had visibly blanched when Hennessy informed him

Christopher & Valerie Share a Lilo
Palm Springs 1969

that 'the trouble with you literary types is you've never had a good giggle'. In Hockney's famous portrait, 'Christopher and Valerie Share a Lilo, Palm Springs, 1969', the signs of marital strain are already appearing. Hennessy's ample bosom seems to hog most of the aforesaid lilo, driving Isherwood, clad only in water-wings, halfway into the pool he so feared. Six weeks later, they were divorced.

Her short stint as editor of the *TLS* was not a happy one, and her inauguration of a 'Ratbag of the Week' section infuriated the higher circles of academia, who disapproved of Sir Isaiah Berlin being described as 'another turgid so-called pen-pusher', and Sir William Golding as 'a hairy old hack with a heart of gold'. Nor did they approve of the lead review being given over to an article in praise of Leonard Cohen by Claire Rayner ('a lovely, lovely man, and a really tremendous poet, bless him, who tells us more about our problems – yours and mine – in one song than a certain William Shakespeare managed in a dozen full-length feature films'). It was time for Val Hennessy to move on.

It must have been during her brief and tempestuous marriage to Sir Harold Acton that I first encountered Miss (Ms!) Hennessy. I had grown accustomed to a delightful annual holiday with Sir Harold in the agree-able surroundings of his *palazzo* in *Firenze*, there to while away those Tuscan evenings with talk of Piero della Francesca, where to find the finest *Cambazola* and the latest slim volume of versification by our old spar-ring-partner A. L. Rowse. It came as something of a surprise, then, when I arrived at aforesaid *palazzo*, wicker-work travelling basket choc-a-bloc with Ben-dick's Bittermints, a bottle or two of a quite exceptional Andalusian *Armagnac* and the latest edition of the Lyt-telton/Hart-Davis Letters, all set for a delightful sojourn of civilised conversation in exquisite company, only to be met by a pouting young puss dressed in a low-cut leotard jiving to the sounds of the Grateful Dead blaring through a personal 'Walkman', as I believe they are termed. This, I realised at once, was not John Julius Norwich.

I cannot, in all honesty, pretend that we 'got on'. Halfway through that evening's estimable repast, the new Lady Acton climbed on to the lap of poor Kenneth Rose and proceeded to lambast Hughie Trevor-Roper, sitting opposite, for his failure to appreciate the love sonnets of Roger McGough. 'Unputdownable, his sonnets are, completely unputdownable!' Poor Kenneth Rose, struggling for breath, looked as if he was finding his hostess a mite unputdownable in her own right. 'The trouble with you guys is,' continued Lady Acton, turning the full force of her ferocity towards Bernie Berenson and the late Diana Cooper, 'you've never had to slog your guts out on the checkout counter at Tesco. Clear off and shovel some shit before you start telling me what's what with books!'

'Ahem,' piped up Sir Harold, 'more *Tortellinni alla Medici*, anyone?' Two weeks later, they were divorced.

And so to Val Hennessy's most recent tome, a collection of her *pensées* upon meeting our contemporary literary giants. It is a formidable appraisal of art in our time, a collection, as she writes of someone else, 'slightly burnished with the shimmer of genius', an intricately woven testament to the continued vitality of the printed word. On the other hand, one can understand why Christopher and Harold found her a bit of a handful. I only hope that her present marriage, to Lord St John of Fawn-Soey, is a little more successful.

MR PAUL JOHNSON

*When Mr Paul Johnson is your guide, you can
be sure that a hearty laugh is never far away!*

*Throughout his oeuvre, Arnold is often drawn to cele-
brate the observations and opinions vouchsafed to readers
of the* Spectator *by the iconoclastic columnist Mr Paul
Johnson. A close personal friend and adviser of Johnson,
Arnold here rejoices in the research undertaken by said
scrivener for the purposes of penning a mould-breaking article
on two subjects close to the hearts of both men: Women and
Humour.*

W.A

I wonder if anyone else read Paul Johnson last week? He
was writing on the subject of humour; home ground,
of course, for this perennial jester. Men and women are
different, he argued. So far, spot on. I, too, have
noticed differences: women have somewhat higher
voices, much given to shrillness, and they dress slightly
oddly too, favouring 'skirts', 'blouses', and so on. But
Paul did not stop there. Women have a different sense
of humour, he said, citing as evidence the fact that few
men can appreciate Mrs T's hilarious 'feminine' jokes,
which, on more than one occasion, have set Johnson
himself a-roar.

Now Johnson is always worth bending an ear for,
and never more so than when talking of mirth. Anyone
who, like me, has had the immense good fortune to
venture into Maison Johnson will have been delighted
to find that the giggling never abates. Morning, noon

and night, the merry cackle of the jovial scribe echoes from the attic room wherein his knockabout jests take shape. Whoopee cushions, water pistols, novelty masks, stink bombs and 'Dirty Fido' memorabilia are scattered hither and thither throughout the public rooms. Following a feast awash with hilarity, Paul launches into his celebrated impersonation of Mr Frank Spencer from the television comedy programme, *Some Mothers Do Have 'Em*, and the old ribs simply ache with laughter.

But too few people realise that Paul also has a serious side. In last week's essay, he touched upon something which is, to my mind, very serious indeed. 'It is significant,' he wrote, 'that men at a striptease show sit in solemn silence whereas women watching a male strip laugh all the time.'

It is by now well known that, aside from his considerable skills as a humorist, Paul is our very best investigative journalist, bar none. Some readers may doubt that a man as industrious and prolific could find time to haunt the striptease bars of darkest Bucks, pen and notebook to hand. But they would be wrong. I feel sure that for months before that sentence was penned, the familiar fiery hair and cheery face of our leading wag could be seen above the saloon-bar smoke at the Thursday lunch strip hour in the Dog and Duck down Iver way, chortling heartily while his *confrères* sat in solemn silence.

To chronicle the reactions of women to a male striptease was altogether trickier. Paul's first stab at infiltration, dressed in wig and mini-skirt borrowed from a great aunt, came to a sticky end. He had forgotten to remove his jacket and tie and was turned away, amidst threats to summon the local constabulary. He was thus forced to go the 'whole hog'. Soon 'Porky Paul' was topping the bill at a hen night in one of Iver's most prestigious nightspots. From the unbutton-

ing of the waistcoat to the throwing down of the
sparkling 'pouch', the assembled ladies laughed until
the tears rolled down their unbristled cheeks. 'For
women,' Paul was now able to write from experience,
'pleasure and laughter are inseparable.'

KEEPER OF THE QUEEN'S PICTURES

An expert among experts!

Wallace Arnold's immense influence on the world of British art is, perhaps, less recognised than his contributions to the spheres of politics, letters and high society. In attempting to redress this balance, the editor of Antique *magazine asked Arnold to shed a little light on his rise to the top, a request that was more than met with this revealing, good humoured and, perhaps above all, art-loving exercise in autobiography.*

W.A.

It was in the spring of 1981 that I was appointed Keeper of the Queen's Pictures, and since that date I have, of course, gone from strength to strength. At the present moment, I am not only the leading architectural adviser to the Duke and Duchess of York, but also the Chief Preservation Supervisor for English Heritage, with special responsibilities for knocking down old buildings. From these lofty heights, it might be inferred with some justification that I know my Picasso from my El Greco, if you'll pardon my *Français*(!!).

Many readers of *Antique* magazine wishing to make a career in Art will want to know how to get a first foot on the proverbial ladder. First, I would tell these little people that they must, above all else, absolutely adore all Art. I myself could spend day upon day walking around some of our leading galleries, simply soaking in the pictures, breathing in their wisdom, their tranquillity, their marvellous sense of texture, of colour, of shape, if only I could spare the time. But one can't afford to waste precious minutes shilly-shallying limp-wristedly around the picture houses when one has the building of a reputation in the world of art to consider. Far from it: a smidgin of elbow-grease in the committee rooms is worth any amount of traipsing about the dusty museums looking 'sincere' (dread word!) as one gawps in the approved manner at one treasure or another.

Enough art theory for the time being, methinks: let us to the autobiography. I first realised that my name was being mooted for the post of Keeper of the Queen's Pictures when I picked up the telephone one morning to find the Duke of Edinburgh, no less, on the other end of the line. At the time, I had been relishing my appointment as Senior Photographic Adviser to the then Prince Andrew, whose snaps of luscious lovelies – young birds of the unfeathered variety, I might add! – had been drawing high praise from royal art circles for their extraordinary ability to capture a moment in time, their use of black and white, and, perhaps above all, for their technical brilliance in fitting most of the subject in question, bar the odd eye, into the picture. My sympathetic help to Prince Andrew – which culminated, I might add, in his excellent set of engagement photographs, 'HRH Prince Andrew and The Left Hand Bit of Miss Sarah Ferguson Pictured At A Slight Slant on the Occasion of their Engagement' – had led the Duke to perceive me as a likely candidate for the plum post. 'Pop round for an informal barbecue cooked by yours truly in the Palace grounds this Sunday, Arnold', he barked down the blower. 'We're having half a dozen other so-called experts round at the same time. We'll be testing you for manners, general conversation, ability with knife and fork, due reverence, and so forth – oh, and you'd better gen up on the Deadly Daubings of the

Dear Departed because they're bound to crop up. Seven for seven-thirty, kebabs at eight prompt.' And with that His Royal Highness replaced His receiver.

★ ★ ★

Outside the Palace gates, into whom should I bump but my old quaffing-partner Mr – later Lord!! – St John Stevas, taking the air with Sir Roymond Strong who, being in public, had donned the moustache-nose-and-specs novelty mask upon which his lofty reputation was based.

'Norman! Roymond!' I exclaimed. 'And what brings you both to these fair parts?'

'We're here for the same reason as you,' replied Roymond, ill-concealing the sharpened daggers with which he looked at me, 'and, no doubt, for the same reason as friend Palumbo over there!'

I looked around and there, in the middle distance, was the unmistakable figure of Mr Peter Palumbo marching towards us, a characteristic swagger in his step. The competition was looking fierce.

'May the best man win,' I graciously interjected while Norman took charge of the doorbell.

'Best man? Best woman, more like!!' came the voice of a late arrival. It was Bubbles, Lady Rothermere, dressed as a kangaroo for a charity launch-party she was to attend later that evening on behalf of Elocution for the Underprivileged. The five candidates having assembled, the gate was opened by the Duke himself, who was armed with a trayful of luke-warm retsina, ready-poured.

'Mmmm! Back to basics! That's the life! Mmmm! Smells good! Nothing better than grilling in the open air! Mmmm! Grab a bun, lads! One, two!' The Duke was in his element as he poked and nudged the sizzling kebabs with a charcoaled twig. Meanwhile, Her Majesty was 'sounding us out', each one in turn, on the subject of Art, behind a neighbouring bush.

'So you're fond of Art, are you?' I overheard her ask Norman.

'Oh, rather!' he replied. 'Delightful young boy!'

'No – *art*,' replied Her Majesty, a testy note entering her tone. 'You know, pictures and furniture.'

Too late for Norman, all conversation was suddenly curtailed by a large burp coming from the direction of Bubbles, Lady Rothermere. It appeared that, unable to wait any longer, she had snaffled a kebab from the barbecue and, after secreting it for a few seconds in her kangaroo pouch, had wolfed it in one gulp only to find that it had 'gone down' the wrong way. 'Whoops! Pardon I!' she apologised, but the rest of us knew instinctively that the damage had already been done to her cause. I'm ashamed to say that I could not forbear but to smile.

With Norman and Bubbles out of the running, I had only to 'see off' Palumbo and Roymond for the post to be mine. While Palumbo was submitting to his cross-questioning by Her Majesty, I wheedled up to Roymond, his kebab now brushing his whiskers, and asked him, *sotto voce*, what he thought of the worst excesses of modern art. 'GHASTLY!' he boomed. 'PERFECTLY DREADFUL! QUITE DISGUSTING!'

Alas for poor Roymond, I had timed my whispered question to coincide with the arrival of the Duke, who was circulating with his flagon of retsina. 'Eh? What was that? What'd'ye say?' he asked dear Roymond, who appeared so taken aback by the Duke's sudden presence that I felt that I should 'chip in' and help him out.

'I had just asked Sir Roymond what he thought of your excellent Doner Kebabs, Your Highness,' I explained, 'and I'm afraid that bluntness is his greatest virtue.'

'B-b-b-but,' spluttered Roymond, but it was too late

for excuses. The Duke had already made his feelings quite clear with a swift kick to his shins. Bitterly upset, Sir Roymond made an early departure, silk handkerchief a-dab-dab-dabbing at his ever-moist eyes.

Mr Peter Palumbo was drawing to the end of a lengthy conversation with Her Majesty, and it seemed to be going quite swimmingly, so I knew that I would have to move fast. 'Might I perchance encroach further upon your generosity Your Highness, by requesting another of your perfectly delectable kebabs, *s'il vous plait*!?' I asked the Duke, who seemed quite delighted at my enthusiasm for his comestibles.

'On or off the skewer?' he said.

'On if I may, Your Highness, many thanks,' I replied.

Skewered kebab in hand, I shimmied over in the direction of Palumbo, leaving the Duke and Norman facing one another in awkwardness, Norman still trying to explain who Art was, the Duke grunting vigorously.

'Your enthusiasm for our Royal collection is positively infectious, Mr Palumbo!' the Queen was saying as I fought my way through the bush behind which Palumbo was standing. I had only seconds to act.

'And do tell me, what do you consider the mark of a great painter?' Her Majesty was now tying up the conversation, so, having moved to within easy reach of Palumbo's posterior, I brandished the aforesaid sizzling skewered kebab and, with one fell swoop, thrust it as far as it would go.

'WAAAAAAAAAAAAARGGGGGHHHHHH!' replied Palumbo to Her Majesty's perfectly reasonable question, before, without so much as a by your leave, rushing headlong into the central lake, ignoring all signs to the contrary and, much to the Duke's consternation, disturbing our web-footed friends.

'Glorious weather we're having for the time of year, ma'am,' I said, stepping out of the bush, and, by her smile alone, I could tell that the post was now mine, all mine.

AYATOLLAH KHOMEINI

A fish out of water

In this remarkable trilogy of memoirs of the Ayatollah Khomeini in the London of the 1960s, Arnold recalls a frustrated soul, at turns shy, aggressive, humourless and charming, motivated by an increasing adherence to the Koran and an interest in skiffle. Though the three pieces – written at different times – all shed myriad lights on this curious character, they are united in their certainty that there was something peculiarly un-English about him.

W.A.

(1)

A most agreeable item in Mr Kenneth Rose's effort-lessly entertaining column in the *Sunday Telegraph*. It appears that the indefatigable Miss Arianna Stassino-poulos is now penning a major tome on 'The Forgotten Years' of the Ayatollah Khomeini, having already completed estimable *oeuvres* on the divine Callas and the dread Picasso. Though I never knew Sophie Khomeini, as he then was, at all well, I knew many who did, especially during his now seemingly 'forgotten' London years in the early 1960s.

Still lacking much direction, Sophie Khomeini would drop in on an almost daily basis to the Colony Room Club to quaff whatever was going with friends of an artistic bent, such as the then unknown Francis Bacon and George Melly. The son of a Persian diplo-

matist and a theatrical costumier from Chiswick, he
even then seemed embarrassed by the supposed effemi-
nacy of his Christian name, preferring the more bluff
and straightforward 'Bill'. It was after his leg had been
pulled just once too often on the subject that he decided
to cultivate his now-famous beard.

Quite what he was doing in the London of the early
Sixties, no one was sure, though it was strongly
rumoured that he was secretly rehearsing a skiffle
group with the likes of Cyril Connolly and the then
unknown Mandy Rice-Davies. But, for one reason and
another, it failed to get off the ground, and this setback
drove him to take a greater and greater interest in
Islamic Fundamentalism, a frustratingly difficult topic
to wheedle into conversation at the Colony in those
days. Of course, the immortal Muriel Belcher would
send him up something rotten. 'Sophie's a little glum
today,' she would bellow from behind her perpetual
glass of bubbly. 'Cat got your tongue, ducks?' While
the rest of us roared with laughter – though, in retros-
pect, I suspect that Paul Johnson, even then, might have
been offended by her flippancy – Khomeini would look
down at his pocket Koran with that broody look in his
eyes. Before long, he let his club subscription pass
unrenewed, and he drifted out of our lives. Perhaps if
we had taken him more seriously, his career would
have taken a rather different turn. As it was, towards
the end of his life he lost touch with most of his old
London cronies, though Mary Kenny reports receiving
the odd postcard, generally of pussy-cats, their shared
love. In a recent photograph, the blurred silhouette of a
skiffle board could be seen on the balcony behind him.
His favourite was always 'Does Your Chewing Gum
Lose Its Flavour on the Bedpost Overnight?', though I
doubt whether this cut much ice with his fellow Kurds.
But I do hope that the delicious Arianna manages to
bring out the latent sense of *joie de vivre* that remains the

'Quite what he was doing in the London of the early Sixties, no one was sure.'

abiding impression many of us have of the Ayatollah who will, to us, always be remembered as just plain Sophie.

★   ★   ★

(II)

The Ayatollah and I first met at a *Private Eye* luncheon in 1968, and even then I could tell he was a wrong 'un. Ingrams's canny eye had alighted upon yours truly as a young and dashing man–about–town who had thankfully failed to succumb to the prevailing liberal ethos of free love, peace, long hair and what–not. At first it seemed that Mr Khomeini, as he then was, and myself saw eye–to–eye on the major issues. He expressed a hearty dislike for Miss (Ms!) Yoko Ono, who was then in vogue, and told the assembled company in no uncertain terms that he would not, repeat, not be going to see the moving picture *Easy Rider*.

So far, so good. He was then a struggling advertising copywriter with J. Walter Thompson, and though his snappy slogans – 'Buy one or expect no mercy' (Playtex Cross–Your–Heart Girdles) and 'Allah be Praised, It's The Best' (Alphabetti Spaghetti) – had failed to gain the approval of his superiors, he seemed an agreeable cove with a languid, if somewhat severe, manner. I remember telling a joke about Simon Dee which seemed to meet with his approval. In fact, he revealed to me that his worst television programme, bar none, was the latter's *Dee Time*. He did not so much laugh as thump and bang on the table, but I could tell that we were agreed on essentials. Ingrams seemed to like him, too. They shared a certain antipathy to Janis Joplin, a debauched American female singer of the time. Ingrams was anxious to get him to contribute to the 'Grovel' column, passing judgement on the fruitier aspects of people's private lives.

Of course, at the time none of us knew a thing of his

politics, still less of his religion, I suppose we must have had him down as a woolly liberal, what with his beard and sandals. He always had a look of Jeremy Thorpe, I seem to remember, and in many ways, he still has.

It was towards the end of our estimable repast at the Coach and Horses that one's hackles began to rise. Ingrams offered him a glass of port, and was understandably taken aback when Khomeini refused, and in no uncertain terms. 'I would cut my own throat with the sword of my grandmother rather than sip of your satanic poison,' he said. 'Only asking,' muttered Ingrams. The rest of us attempted to make light of this remark, but luncheon frittered to a close shortly afterwards.

A year or two later, we heard that Khomeini had been handed his cards by J.W.T. after suggesting posting death threats upon all those who refused to purchase 'Crazy Foam', a soap-based novelty fluid then in vogue. A decade on, much to our great surprise, he emerged as top dog in Iran, his mirthless visage often in the papers. Now Rushdie has put his foot in it – whoops! – but it is Simon Dee for whom I really feel frightened. Will he now apologise for *Dee Time*? For his own sake, I do hope so.

★   ★   ★

(III)

Over the past few months, I have found cause to emphasise the need for a sense of humour. If one cannot laugh at oneself, one is almost bound to 'take a tumble'. I have many foibles and failings which I am only too happy to chortle at. I am thinking now of my reckless generosity, my too rigorous adherence to a strict code of personal morality, my genuine love of people. 'Oh Wallace!' I sometimes say to myself as the night draws in, 'you really are the most lovable scamp!' And it is this ability to laugh at myself that has, I believe, seen me through thick and thin.

My thoughts returned to the subject when I heard of the death this weekend past of the Ayatollah Khomeini of that parish. He may have been a remarkable old gent in many ways (it took some nerve, I would imagine, to wear such a flamboyant beret, especially at his ripe old age) but I rather suspect that he had little or no sense of humour. Hence that famous down-in-the-mouth expression he chose to employ, even in prime-time news programmes, and hence his extraordinary propensity for getting in an awful flap about nothing. Though a sworn teetotaller, he would have done well to sup the tonic of humour.

I knew him only a little when he was exiled to London in the late 1960s (loathsome decade!). Bill Davies had taken something of a shine to Khomeini, having met him at the launch of *Funny Old World: a Century of British Humour*, and had immediately offered him the plum job of cartoon editor on *Punch* magazine. Alas, few cartoons inspired even the mildest of smirks on that grizzled visage, though I seem to remember him chuckling at the priceless antics of the Gambols in Barry Appleby's strip cartoon of the same name. By and large, he felt that no cartoon that failed to reflect his own devout belief in Islam should pass muster, and consequently *Punch* fell into a circulation spiral from which it is still struggling to recover. *The Punch Book of Praise to Allah* published at the end of that year, suffered from poor sales, alas.

I suspect that I have inadequately stressed the poor sense of humour that formed such a dominant part of his somewhat prickly character. I well remember him popping his head around the door to bid his old mess-mates ta-ra at the *Punch* offices, just prior to his return to Iran in 1979. 'It'll be awfully dry over there,' I quipped, 'now that the Shower of Rain has departed!

No need for wellies, eh?!!' He shot me one of his grimmest looks, and, as I sat there explaining the delicious pun (Shah/Shower – Iran/Rain), he stomped off in a bate.

He never looked very happy out there, to my mind, poor chap. Perhaps it was the climate, perhaps the responsibility. But I rather think that, with a sense of humour, he would have learnt to enjoy himself. May his example be a lesson to us all. There's no medicine like laughter, methinks.

MR C. S. LEWIS

The secret life of an Oxford legend

*A*nn Wilson, the novelist and biographer, is a constant *figure in the writings of Arnold, leading some to suppose that their relationship went beyond the purely academic. Nevertheless, the undoubted affection that exists between them never allows Arnold to turn a blind eye to Ann's faults. In a masterly piece written to coincide with the publication of Ann Wilson's biography of C. S. 'Jack' Lewis, which exposed her subject's sex-life to unprecedented scrutiny, Arnold suggests that there are revelations still to be uncovered.*

W.A.

Second to none in my appreciation of Miss (Ms!) Ann Wilson, I only hope that her new biography of C. S. Lewis will not be thoroughly overshadowed by my own first-hand account of the man, *Wallace and Jack*, to be published next week.

Ever the busy bee, Ann has been diligent in grubbing around in the mud, and, sure enough, she has discovered that Jack Lewis 'led a double life', replacing top on Parker '45 betwixt penning paragraphs on *The Problem of Pain* in order to bicycle posthaste to a Miss Marilyn Monroe, then lodging in digs somewhere beyond Magdalen Bridge, there to have his wicked way.

Such prurience in a biographer is to be roundly condemned. It may well be that there are those who wish to have their reading of *The Lion, The Witch and*

The Wardrobe sullied by visions of an erotic whirlwind of discarded bicycle clips but I am not among them. My own, more personal, reminiscence recalls Jack as he was: a bachelor don, distinguished in a tremendous variety of fields, as much a friend of the saloon bar as of the common room, full of earthy good humour and (occasionally caustic!) observation, a man imbued from top to toe with Christian understanding, a theologian, a literary critic and a part-time cabaret artiste in the risqué Pussy Galore Club in Old Compton Street. My own affectionate memoir concentrates on this latter, perhaps less well-known aspect of Jack's immensely varied career, an aspect all but missing from Ann's now hopelessly outmoded effort in poison-pennery.

From Miss Monroe's digs on the far side of Magdalen Bridge, Jack would don nose-specs-and-moustache novelty mask to bicycle without fear of recognition to the railway station, there to catch the fast train to Paddington. Once aboard, he would meet his fellow Inklings – J. R. R. Tolkien (double bass), Neville Coghill (bassoon), Charles Williams (keyboards) and H. V. D. Dyson (maracas) – and, in the closely-guarded privacy of the guard's van they would rehearse that night's performance, with Jack Lewis going full throttle on vocals.

Oh, we think things
'Cos we're the Ink-lings
And we're always wink-ing
Yes, we're the I-N-K-L-I-N-G-S
– INKLINGS!!!

The gusto and sheer toe-tapping bonhomie of this witty, fast-moving intro may lose a little in print but on stage the effect was electrifying, the number gaining greatly from Professor Tolkien's undisputed mastery of the kazoo. But alas, the days of variety were already in decline and the more glamorous and up-to-date (dread phrase!) combination of the Beverley Sisters – females all three – soon supplanted the Inklings. Of the original Inklings, only F. P. J. ('Frankie') Vaughan found fame in show business; the rest sought succour in the more dry and dusty world of academe. In ignoring this other, even more secret life, Ann has, I fear, failed to grasp the essence of the man.

LIVERPOOL

Let's not duck the awkward questions!

It has been said of Wallace Arnold that he is as happy to take tea with the Queen as to place a modest Christmas 'box' in a strategic place for collection by a goodly dustman. Here, soon after the Hillsborough tragedy, he demonstrates his very real interest in the affairs of 'ordinary people' by recalling a visit he himself once made to the great city of Liverpool.

W.A.

In that most civilised of journals, the *Independent* magazine (what other magazine, in these modern days, is brave enough to be so dull?), my eyes chanced upon a most appealing article previewed in the justly renowned table of contents. 'HOME THOUGHTS' ran the intriguing title, with, underneath, the following summary: 'Andrew Gimson refuses to duck awkward questions arising out of football's latest tragedy.'

Brave man, Gimson! I have little doubt that, upon hearing Gimson was penning a piece on football's latest tragedy, the bigwigs in the Football Association, in league with the City Councils and Chambers of Commerce of Sheffield and Liverpool, were on the blower in seconds, pleading with the doughty scrivener to duck the awkward questions. But Gimson is made of stronger stuff than that. Canny observer of the human heart that he is, he pinned the blame for football's latest tragedy fairly and squarely on the common little tykes who find that muddy, mindless 'game' in the least bit interesting, and quite right too. 'The worst condescension of all,' he concluded, 'would be to suggest that they do not have only themselves to blame.'

Like Gimson, I too have earned the trust of the proud citizens of the great city of Liverpool. I was lucky enough to be there for well over five minutes after a misreading of the road map as recently as 1961. 'Oy,' I said, adopting native parlance as I leaned out of the front window of my automobile. 'Oy! Mate! Could you kindly set me on a road appropriate to the swiftest of all possible exits from this estimable conglomeration of buildings known as Liverpool? Good on yer! Mate!'

I could tell immediately that I had won the fellow over. As luck would have it, I had also run him over, my brakes being what they were, and I was therefore forced to avail myself of the services of another goodly wayfarer, who shook his fist at me in the jovial proud manner so characteristic of the region. The city, I realised at once, had taken Wallace Arnold to its heart.

No ducker of questions, I therefore speak direct to the trusty folk of Liverpool via the pages of the *Spectator*, like a mother hen speaking to her chicks, and I trust my remarks will not be seen as in the least bit patronising.

The message of Wallace Arnold is this: listen carefully to what Mr Gimson has to say, and brood on it. When he tells of the greater pleasures to be gained from a perusal of Jane Austen than from the rough and tumble of the soccer pitch, he knows that about what he speaks. 'Gimmers' has been around a bit – Malta, Tuscany, North Cornwall – and the bruises he has gained thereby have garnered his complete lack of condescension. May his suggestion to convert the Kop into an emporium for the finest of International Ballet bear fruit, and thus avert another tragedy.

MR HAROLD MACMILLAN

*W*hen the Editor of the Literary Review *required someone to review Alistair Horne's official biography of Harold Macmillan, the first person he turned to was, of course, Wallace Arnold. His first-hand experience of the so-called 'Night of the Long Knives', together with his outstanding ability to paint vivid word-pictures, have led many to wonder why he himself, some ten years previously, had turned down the job later awarded to Horne.*

W.A.

Extraordinary times, indeed. Satire, ugly beast, was raising its tawdry head, and sex, as per u., was never far behind. In an otherwise magnificent celebration of our most bookish and civilised of Prime Ministers, Alistair Horne nevertheless fails to answer the question of the Headless Man. Some say he was that well-loved comedian Arthur Askey, others hothead philosopher Bertrand Russell, still others the popular quizmaster Mr Michael Miles. I doubt very much indeed whether the aforesaid gentleman was our own Prince Philip, for, in younger, flightier days, I had cause to glimpse HRH 'in the buff', as it were, and nowhere on the body portrayed in the infamous photo is there a tattoo bearing the legend 'I love Mum', the original 'B' having been skilfully overlaid. Some of the rumours are, to my mind, way off – Alexander Solzhenitsyn, for instance, was simply not around at the time – but others have

'Living proof that the morality of days gone by was by no
means a thing of the past.'

about them a pleasing ring of truth. Noel Coward, the Master himself? Hardly. Rolf Harris? Too young. Gilbert Harding? Bill Haley? Mr Pastry? Maybe, maybe.

The very mention of those names manages to conjure up an era long since past. 'You've never had it so good,' said the great statesman at a meeting of the Inner Cabinet one day, little realising that most of them had hot-footed it from one of Margaret, Duchess of Argyll's coffee-mornings. As the blood rushed to their cheeks, Macmillan continued to rattle on, quite unaware of the hornets' nest of licentiousness and adultery that was buzzing so very close to the reins of power.

But first things first, Wallace, first things first. A mere stripling of a lad, I had the immense privilege of serving under Big Mac as general office boy in Number Ten, and I have good cause to remember what a very civilised and, perhaps above all, well-read man he was. As Horne makes clear, the so-called 'Night of the Long Knives' pained him deeply, but he took solace in literature.

I remember the scene as if it were yesterday. In the Outer Waiting Room, half the Cabinet sat, sombre and tense, waiting for their marching orders. They had been summoned from whatever it was they were doing with no warning whatsoever. Some were still in their posing pouches, others had had no time to remove their serving-wench get-ups, others had hastily thrown on whatever clothes were at hand – a mistake, I fear, as Selwyn Lloyd, to my mind, had quite a fight on his hands in order to retain his composure while dolled-up in a strapless 'Baby-Doll' nightie.

Inside the Prime Minister's office, Macmillan looked grim-faced indeed, seeming to take solace in his beloved books. 'You may be wondering why I've summoned you here this evening' he said, barely looking up at Lord Hill while he reached for a slim volume of Mediaeval Verse. 'I must admit I was rather, Harold,

old man,' said Lord Hill, the croak of terror alive in his
quaking voice. The awful time had come, and Harold
had no option but to go through with it, for the good of
the nation as a whole. But he did it with such charm and
discretion, with such bookish, olde-worlde dignity,
mixing civilised *aperçus* with his sadder tidings, that
Lord Hill took it all in good part.

'Marvellous fellow, Chaucer,' began Macmillan,
flicking through an extract from *Troilus and Criseyde*,
'such robust, earthy humour, such insight into the
highs and lows of common humanity, now get lost,
Hill, and don't darken this doorstep again, such broad
poetic sweeps, resonant down the centuries!' It was a
masterly dismissal, executed with Macmillan's brilliant
timing and lightness of touch. There were a few tears
from Hill, of course there were, but, hearing his dismissal couched in such gloriously civilised language,
even he seemed strangely elated, adjusting his tutu with
great dignity as he strode out, never to return.

As the white-hot winds of change swept through this
once-great land of ours, Big Mac seemed a reassuring
anchor, living proof that the morality of days gone by
was by no means a thing of the past. His ready wit had
about it an anachronistic flavour. 'And tell me, boy,
what might this be?' I once overheard him ask his
chauffeur, as he stood on the steps of Downing Street.
'Your car, M'Lud,' replied the chauffeur. 'Car? Car?
And what on earth is a car?' asked Macmillan. 'A four-
wheeled vehicle propelled by a motor, M'Lud,' replied
the chauffeur. 'Good Lord,' exclaimed Macmillan, 'and
what do you expect me to do with it?' 'Ride in it,
M'Lud.' 'Anything you say, anything you say,' said
Macmillan, hitching up his tails and climbing on to the
roof-rack. 'Ready when you are.' Quite possibly, this is
the last time the nation will ever witness a Prime
Minister travelling up the Mall to the palace sitting,
albeit with great dignity, on the roof of his vehicle.

Golden days, indeed, and recorded with admirable verve by Alistair Horne. I trust that a subsequent volume will deal more fully with the question of the headless man. It could not have been Gandhi, as he was a vegetarian, and dead, to boot. My own crisp oncer remains on Askey, for all his *faux naif* talk of buzzy bees, etcetera.

THOSE MARVELLOUS MITFORDS

A touch of lovable eccentricity never goes amiss when dealing with Those Marvellous Mitfords!

All twenty-three Mitford sisters have come, over the years, to see Wallace Arnold as their natural friend and confidant. Other biographers may have been more scholarly, more 'gritty', more no-holds-barred, but only Arnold has, for them, fully understood the delicious whit and whimsies of the gloriously aristocratic. Here, he provides an invaluable vignette *concerning the role of the biographer.*

W.A.

I have long favoured maroon socks, and I am occasionally attracted by the prospect of sweet sherry, but in few other ways am I what one might describe as eccentric. Nevertheless, the avowedly eccentric have long seen in me a soul-mate. They recognise me, I suspect, as a 'people person', delighting in the foibles of my fellow man, collecting them as others collect trinkets or stamps.

My library of commonplace books, stretching back now over 30 odd years, provides an at-a-glance guide to the peccadilloes and partialities of the unconventional.

I need hardly state how invaluable these commonplace books have proved while I have been compiling *Those Marvellous Mitfords*, an anthology of the antics and aphorisms of that peculiarly British family, to be published by My Lord Weidenfeld in the spring.

Over the past week, section M for Mitford has grown full to o'erflowing, for I have had the immense good fortune to bump into Decca, the most radical of the famous sisters, who founded her own recording company before flying to China to fight for Che Guevara against Franco. Now, as gloriously leftish as ever, she never enters a London taxi without first offering to share the driving.

Regaling me with hilarious tales of Farv, Muv, their ill-trained butler, Shuv, and their nouveau-riche governess, Parv, Decca Mitford insisted I join the family for an intensely personal reunion amidst the intimate surroundings of a Foyle's Literary Luncheon. I accepted with glee.

The entire Mitford clan was present, except, I am sorry to say, Diana, whom Decca had refused to invite for fear she would use the occasion to rally fellow diners against the duly elected democratic government. But it was most agreeable to see Debo, dressed casually in the barest modicum of tiaras, and the other one, whose name few could remember, but who appears very much alive. 'Wallace Arnold, allow me to introduce you to my sister . . . Erm . . . Erm . . . ' said Decca. 'Delighted to meet you, Erm,' I chipped in, quick as a flash, saving everyone much embarrassment.

It was an especial pleasure to make the acquaintance of the younger generation of Mitfords. Across the table from me was the anorexic Pecca, habitually toying with her food. In a corner, flirting with a sous–chef, was Necca. Hacksaw in hand, daubing slogans in blancmange on the restaurant walls, was the anarchistic Recca. Finally, under the table, performing the midday worshipping rites of her beloved Kurdish fundamentalist sect, came young Mecca, the first full-blooded Muslim Mitford. Sadly, the only brother, Becca, was away playing tennis at the time.

From this delightful encounter with the Mitfords *en masse*, I consider myself a changed man, a man much more able to revel in his own idiosyncracies. I am searching for a suitably outlandish cigarette holder, have taken to wearing slip-on shoes and speak animatedly of my preference for the colour pink. Already I am creating quite a stir. We English, you see, simply *love* a true eccentric.

GENERAL MANUEL NORIEGA

The Garrick years

*W̶hile the deposed General Manuel Noriega of Panama
was being bombarded with rock music by troops wishing to flush him out of his refuge in the Vatican embassy,
Arnold wrote this considered appreciation – wry, informed
and never less than affectionate – of the man whose election to
the Garrick Club he had once effected.*

W.A.

It was with no little regret that, while casting my eye
o'er the list of members who had expressed their intention of resigning from the Garrick Club, I came across
the name of Noriega, Gen. Manuel, just one down
from Noakes, John. Of course, in recent years he has
been able to muster precious little time to pop his head
around the portals of the club – though I am told that he
put our reciprocal arrangement with the Cavalry and
Pump-Action Shotgun Club, Panama, to good use –
but in his present situation his hopes of swapping Tales
from the Green Room with some of our most illustrious thespians in a small but light-hearted gathering
around the Garrick hall fire seem, frankly, a mite wee.

I remember well the time – it must have been late '67,
early '68 – when the young Manuel Noriega, then
cutting something of a dash as a stringer for the estimable Peterborough column on the *Telegraph*,
approached me, even then a distinguished Man of

Letters, with a view to securing him membership.
Though already afflicted with a by no means inconsiderable skin problem – my espousal of a goodly dash of
Clearasil went unheeded, I fear – Noriega exuded a sort
of rugged charm and devil-may-care enthusiasm which
I for one found positively infectious. 'You make me
Garrick member, I no kill your mama,' he quipped,
over a perfectly acceptable glass o' port in the RAC, of
which he was already making quite a name for himself
as Joint Chairman – with the young David Astor, as
then was – of the Adult Movies Committee. 'No need,'
I countered. 'Dead already!'

We both had a good chuckle over that one, I
remember, and by the very next week I was introducing him to all the leading Garrick bigwigs, among them
the leading theatrical impresario Mr Paul Raymond,
the distinguished comedy actor Mr Reg Varney and the
young George Weidenfeld, then earning an immensely
pocketable sum as a part-time tap-dancer at
Quaglino's.

Duly elected, Manuel took to the club like the proverbial feathered biped to H_2O, and it was after listening
to the after-dinner banter of Mr Terry Worsthorne that
he set his heart upon becoming a Supreme Head of
State. Posted back to Panama for a few weeks by the
top guns on Peterborough with a view to his spying out
humorous road-signs and ticklish menu translations, he
grasped the opportunity to parade about the sun-
soaked streets in his Garrick Club tie, thus gaining the
respect of the military junta of the time. It then took
only one or two appropriately placed retellings of
backstage anecdotes concerning Johnny Gielgud and
his sieve-like memory(!) for Manuel to be accepted as
one of their own by the Panamanian High Command.
The rest, as they say, is history. One small footnote,
though. Sad as I am at his resignation, I cannot help but

breathe a sigh of relief. Had he perchance sought sanc-
tuary in the Garrick, the endless barrage of the cater-
waulings of pop (dread word!) 'musicians' would, I
fear, be rather more than one could reasonably bear.

THE OXFORD ENGLISH DICTIONARY

Words galore!

N*o slouch himself when it comes to words, Arnold here pays fulsome tribute to a mammoth undertaking by a great many little people.*

W.A.

A veritable monument to our Island Tongue; a treasure trove of etymological delight and elucidation; the greatest novel ever written; a vast sweeping river, wherein all fish are words; a Forth Road Bridge, spanning words both great and small, upon which the paint never sets; a delightful concatenation of the learned and the – ah, but how can one ever begin to praise the new *Oxford English Dictionary*? I could not have become a writer without it, still less a verbal craftsman, a juggler with words, an internationally renowned purveyor of finely honed sentences, paragraphs, chapters and – yes! – tomes.

Of course, one never has cause to use the damn thing, but that in no way detracts from its stately magnificence. If I ever wanted to know what on earth 'cling-film' might be, and I have little reason to suppose that such a circumstance would ever arise(!), I would save myself time by quizzing the little woman on the 'check-out counter', presuming I knew what on earth a 'check-out counter' was. To consult Bob Burchfield's massive oracle, gloriously ungainly and inaccessible as it is, would waste precious hours, and I rather suspect that it would attempt to tease me into thinking that 'cling-film' was a type of throat lozenge, a form of African gnu or a set of Druidical stones before finally vouchsafing me the requisite information. But the mere detailing of the meaning of words is never the business of a dictionary, gracious me, no. A dictionary is much, much more than that: an attractive piece of furniture, an ice-breaker at parties, a vital companion to BBC television's excellent *Call My Bluff* programme upon which I am so often a guest, with, I am told, no little success. Surveys suggest that, of the 1,500 *Oxford English Dictionaries* that have been printed, only two will ever be consulted, and one of these will be so honoured only because its doughty inquisitor will be in search of a railway timetable for the Euston–Carlisle early morning run. But this, we all agreed at last week's launch party at Claridge's, in no way detracts from the work's outstanding contribution to Western civilisation.

The party was a most agreeable affair. Uncle Bob Burchfield had had the bright idea of getting the glum boffins to 'let their hair down' by allotting half of them 'new words' and the other half 'definitions', and then seeing how quickly they could 'pair off'. Roy Jenkins ('Nerd') spent much of the evening chatting with Kenneth Rose ('Gunge') before locating his definition on the back of Hugh Trevor-Roper ('Daft Twat'). 'Has anyone seen Bonk?' asked Queen Elizabeth the Queen Mother of Sir Roy Strong ('Slagheap') before locating her Bonk on Quintin Hogg, who was chatting animatedly to Anthony Burgess ('Poke'). By the by, the name of Wallace Arnold is renowned among lexicographers as a vital source of the latest developments in the English language; indeed, *Spectator* readers would learn

rather more about how to use words from a period
with the back numbers of 'Afore Ye Go' than by
shelling out £1,500 for this supreme work of the 20th
century, methinks.

MR ENOCH POWELL

Master of fuzzy-felt

The most brilliant mind of one generation is saluted by the most brilliant mind of another generation: the years shall not divide them!

W.A.

'Look upon him. Learn from him. You shall not see his like again.' Paddy Cosgrave's stirring tribute to Enoch manages to hit the nail upon its uppermost protuberance. Enoch and I go back yonks, and we have learnt much from one another. The most brilliant mind of his generation, Enoch is remembered among his contemporaries at kindergarten for the shrewd logic he brought to the game of Grandmother's Footsteps. 'Might I enquire, perchance, in what way or manner the person the back of whose body is facing, as it were, towards me, is to be considered to be wholly or partly my *grandmother*, a term which, in the deepest traditions of our Island tongue, is generally held to represent some direct link of blood, bones and flesh with either the mother of one's father or the mother of one's mother, neither of which appellations, I would venture, can be applied to the aforesaid impostor, and I do not use such a word lightly,' exclaimed the six-year-old Enoch, but by this time his playmates had moved on to hopscotch.

By the age of eight, Enoch was translating 'Humpty Dumpty' into Hindustani, lecturing post-graduates on

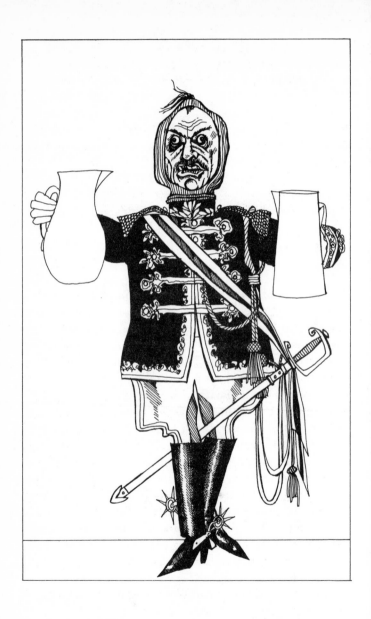

'The great man fixed me with his penetrating stare and asked me which alcoholic beverage I cared to imbibe.'

the dire consequences for the original inhabitants of Old MacDonald's farm of the enforced cohabitation of ducks, donkeys and cows, and applying his rigorous logic to the problems encountered by 'The Three Marys' in the long-running *Bunty* comic strip. By his 12th birthday, sporting the full insignia of the 19th-century Prussian cavalry he so admired, he could be seen at weekends pacing the streets of Nuneaton badgering the goodly populace into taking part in the reconquering of Croydon, a district he believed to have been annexed to Nuneaton in the early 6th century.

I myself first made the acquaintance of this brilliant intellect at a drinks party he gave to celebrate the anniversary of the Battle of Balaclava. Clad in the appropriate head-dress, his moustache just visible through the mouth-hole, the great man fixed me with his penetrating stare and asked me which alcoholic beverage I cared to imbibe. I asked for a gin and tonic. With impeccable logic, he arrived back with two beakers, one filled with gin, the other with tonic. 'You made no mention whatsoever within the terms of your initial request that the two fluids should be mixed in any way,' he answered my protestations, his spurs playing havoc with the carpet as he spoke.

A world authority on macramé, a leading figure in the world of fuzzy-felt, it is probable that he let his passion for the life and works of Herb Alpert and His Tijuana Brass interfere with his political ambitions, often cancelling meetings with heads of state for another chance to hear 'Spanish Flea' on his portable gramophone. Had he been less addicted to the Latin-American rhythms of this veritable master of brass, I have no doubt that Enoch would have proved one of our very greatest of prime ministers.

PUNCH *MAGAZINE*

A heavy-hearted farewell

In this touching elegy to the magazine he so loved, Arnold looks back on many years of healthy tomfoolery and civilised wit. This piece is notable in that it conveys a sense of hurt Arnold is normally adept at concealing from the general reader.

W.A.

It was nigh on 20 years ago that I acceded to the post of Motoring Editor of *Punch* magazine, then under the splendidly eccentric rule of that veritable master of mirth, Bill Davis. So it was with heavy heart that I handed in my resignation last week, sorry (and not a little angry) to know that I was leaving that pleasing periodical, that jovial companion of so many fireside hours, in the hands of ghastly young 'executives', with between them not a spotty pocket handkerchief nor a cravat (two garments which, I have found over the years, are sure signs of a sense of humour).

But bitterness does not, I am glad to say, flow through my veins. This piece is intended to be a celebration of what was – the giggles of helpless laughter as Bill set us all a-hoot with one of his perfectly timed 'knock-knock' jokes, the out-and-out howls that greeted every blissful word of Hunter Davies's ribald tales of family life – and not a condemnation of those colourless marketing types who seek to destroy all that is worthwhile in our culture.

O'er the years I have garnered a splendid collection of humorous anecdotes, simply from being surrounded by some of the most amusing characters in the world. Libby Purves, for instance. Now, there, as our American cousins would say, is one helluva funny lady. She would always arrive on the dot of 11, consummately hilarious piece on, say, 'Problems with Plumbing' or 'A Sideways Look at Baby Rearing' in hand, ever ready with a glorious one-liner, such as – bliss – 'I'm not sure I want to join any club that would have me as a member!!!' Dot Parker, as Bill might say, eat your heart out!

One of the many highlights of my long and varied career on that Powerfully Potty Publication (alas no more) was the launch of the long-awaited *Punch Book of Motoring* edited by Wally Arnold. One and all in that Crazy Crew of *Punch* scribblers had contributed their 1,000-word howlers – Sherry Morley on 'Losing My Way to the Theatre', that Crown Jester Alan Coren on 'How Ernest Hemingway Might Have Written About Getting Into a Hatchback with TV Star David Bellamy – and then Negotiating Spaghetti Junction!', Roy 'The Hat' Hattersley on 'Amusing Moments Motoring in Yorkshire', Hunter Davies on 'But Dad – We're Clean out of Petrol!' and Rob Buckman on 'Doctor, There's a Fly in My Engine!' We held the launch party in, I kid you not, a car showroom – with predictably disastrous results! The image most powerfully fixed in my 'little grey cells' is that of David Taylor walking around with a steering wheel attached to his head, asking wit and raconteur Christopher Matthew if he knew a decent garage! Fare thee well, Mr Punch, fare thee well . . .

HRH QUEEN ELIZABETH THE QUEEN MOTHER

A most loyal and devoted friend!

In 1989, Arnold accompanied the Queen Mother on her visit to the East End. In public, he tends to play down his deep friendships with many senior members of the Royal Family, but here puts his understandable reticence to one side in order to pay tribute to an old lady in whose heart he holds a most precious place.

W.A.

There has always been a special nook in the Queen Mother's heart for the cheery inhabitants of London's East End. When she last visited Rotherhithe in 1941, she was so overcome with affection for the cheery folk that she vowed there and then that she would definitely return within the next 48 years.

True to her word, the nation's favourite great-gran made that onerous trip to Rotherhithe last week. Together with Sir Roy Strong and Mr Kenneth Rose, I enjoyed the immense privilege of being in attendance. It was an experience I am never likely to forget.

'Now I can look the East End in the face,' she had said, all those years ago, after one of her corgis, too, had narrowly missed suffering a not inconsiderable hurt from flying shrapnel, and those cheery, salt-of-the-earth types never forgot it, gor' bless 'em. For they realise, as few people do, quite how tough life has been for this lovely, lovely lady, 88 years young. Early on in life, she received a severe blow when her husband suffered the grave misfortune of acceding to the throne of Britain. Now carrying the burden of Queenship, she had to move her possessions lock, stock and barrel to the agoraphobic conditions of Buckingham Palace, and she is still unable to go anywhere without a full retinue of servants. But this noble lady, never more radiant, has triumphed over all the setbacks life has dealt her, and is always willing to pass on a word of encouragement to the ordinary, common, cheery folk who so idolise her.

The wit of the lady is, of course, legendary. Every page of Robert Lacey's superb critical biography, *The Queen of All Our Hearts*, and its follow-up, *God Bless You Ma'am*, sparkles with a shining gem. And last week in Rotherhithe that comic tongue was one again on top form. 'Raining isn't it, Wallace?' she said to me as we motored along, adding, as quick as a flash, 'I hope we've brought the umbrella!'

I was honoured to be personally deputed to muster as many cheery Eastenders as possible to greet Her Majesty. Marvellous folk all, they are forever popping in and out of each other's two-up, two-downs bearing stews concocted from nutritious scraps, tap-dancing, playing 'spoons', indulging in a little good old-fashioned 'pick-pocketing' and talking to one another in rhyme. Alas, I was informed that most of 'em now live in Harlow New Town, but a large, jubilant crowd of roughly six gathered to pay homage to their own dear Queen Mum. 'Gissa kiss,' yelled one – possibly a 'Pearly King' in civvies. 'Everyone is so very natural here,' quipped back Her Majesty, to universal delight.

Able to speak to all classes, she retains a fondness for the British Pub, and, recognising one – The Old Service Station – she insisted upon an unscheduled stop.

'"Everyone is so natural here" quipped her Majesty, to universal delight.'

'Half of your very best,' she asked the pump attendant, and before long she was sipping a jar of Duckham's to her heart's content. A magical day spent with a magical, magical lady.

ANY QUESTIONS

How democracy came to Little Snodgrass!

*T*hough *he would be loath to say it himself, for the past fifteen years Wallace Arnold has been among the most popular panellists on the long-running* Any Questions *radio programme. Here, in a sparkling piece of reportage, he takes us 'behind the scenes' at the 40th anniversary edition. Note how well he gets on with the VIPs on the show, even though some do not share his firmly held political convictions.*

W.A.

Flattered? Just a trifle. When I first appeared on *Any Questions* fifteen years ago, I had little idea that I would become one of the best-loved members of that outstanding *coterie* of men and, yes, women who are prepared to travel to Little Snodgrass(!!!!) or wherever to tell a village hall full of ordinary, decent folk exactly where we stand on certain issues. And I was indeed flattered to be invited to partake in the 40th anniversary edition of that estimable programme, representing culture, philosophy and common sense on a panel that also comprised Roy Hattersley, Dr David Owen and my old friend Lord Young.

I find that people are always fascinated by what goes on prior to transmission on what used to be the Home Service. While the 200 or so villagers shuffle their feet and blow on their gnarled hands, the four panellists tuck into a sumptuous repast within the warm and well-barricaded confines of the Village Hall. Prior to the 40th anniversary edition, Dr Owen talks cuff-links with David Young, who has a private collection, whilst Roy and I bury our political differences in order to compliment one another on the particular charms of our skills as occasional essayists. 'I always maintain,' observes Roy, 'that an occasional essay should be as delicate yet profoundly uplifting as a well-cooked souf-flé.' I congratulate Roy on his marvellous use of the word 'profoundly' in so many of his essays and speeches: pure Priestley. 'Talking of soufflé,' continues Roy, 'I appear to have finished mine. I would pro-foundly admire seconds, as it happens.'

Come 8.20, the plates are cleared, the silverware put into safekeeping, and the cheery populace shepherded in, visibly moved to find themselves in the presence of such distinguished company. While the first questioner asks us to comment on the authenticity (or otherwise!) of the Turin Shroud, Roy removes a pre-cooked steak and kidney pie from his jacket pocket and kindly offers me a sliver. 'Pass it on,' he whispers, but by this time Dr Owen has launched into a considered reply. 'Let's not beat about the bush on this one,' he says, before telling an enraptured audience of his time as Foreign Secretary.

David Young declares that the question raises very serious issues, particularly in regard to this Govern-ment's long overdue privatisation of British Steel, whilst Roy argues that the present administration is profoundly undemocratic and profoundly arrogant. I myself put forward a strong case for harsher sentences for first-time offenders. 'At the moment, we seem to care more for the criminal than for his innocent victim,' I declare, to hearty applause. 'I hope that answers your question,' says the young Dimbleby to the middle-aged housewife who asked it. She declares that she was fascinated by the range of replies, and is herself in two minds about the Turin Shroud. On the platform, we smile sympathetically.

THE RUSHDIE AFFAIR

Dread words!

*In this long and considered analysis of the popular colum-
nist's response to the Rushdie Affair, Arnold sets out to
show how one skilled political commentator managed to tackle
the political, ethical and social problems in a trenchant yet
sympathetic manner.*

W.A.

I very much doubt whether readers of this column –
many of whom, I am reliably informed, do their level
best to plough their way through the rest of this
eminently civilised journal! – ever have found themselves with time enough to peruse the *Daily Mail*. If this
is the case, might I recommend a change of habit?
Though choc-a-bloc with pampered poodles from the
world of 'entertainment' (dread word!) and much given
to Diets and Duchesses, it also has an illustrious set of
political columnists and opinion-formers, of whom, I
am happy to say, Wallace Arnold 'The Man They Can't
Gag' is one.

Every Wednesday, I offer my hard-hitting opinions
on topical matters to a readership anxious to ascertain
what to think. One week, I might steer them towards a
distaste for homosexuals, whilst the next week will see
me sticking up for those good, old-fashioned virtues of
patriotism and personal hygiene. I also try to 'lighten
the load' with my idiosyncratic and oft tendentious
(words, I regret to say, well above the heads of most

Mail readers!) observations on the minutiae (and there's another!!) of everyday life. The infernal noise of the 'Walkman', the ghastly misuse of the good old English adjective 'gay', the prevalence of 'canned music' in restaurants, the gobbledegook that pours through one's letterbox from left-infiltrated councils: all these have come in for a drubbing at the hands of Arnold, whose sideways look at the world has become a byword for wisdom among the middle and lower-middle classes of the land.

I also possess an enviable gift for extracting amusement from the little difficulties life so often throws in one's path. Whene'er I am afforded poor service in a restaurant, sloppy treatment by an airline, rudeness at the hands of a government employee or a late arrival by British Rail, I make quite sure that my readers come to hear of it, in terms both jocular and trenchant. Only the other day, I marched up to a 'supermarket' counter with an item for purchase and the young lady said, 'Sorry, this counter is closed'!!! With a liberal application of the Wit of Wallace, this made for an entertaining and waspish couple of paragraphs towards the bottom of my page, and I feel sure that it struck a chord in many a less literate reader! I pride myself on being able to put into words those things which the Ordinary Bloke has oft felt but never bothered to say, and if that is not a definition of what good writing is all about, I would very much like to hear what is.

But life is not always easy for a pungent columnist like myself. One must always be on the look-out for a new opinion, whether it be a solution to the Arab/Israeli conflict or a 'put-down' of Aids sufferers. Many people will now be yearning to hear how one managed to keep one's opinions on the Rushdie Affair provocative and challenging these twelve months past.

'Wallace Arnold is a man who knows his own mind' read my application for the UK Press Awards. Might I now, in all humility, show you how this mind tackled just one of the great issues of our day?

Looking at my files, I see that, after January 14th of last year, when a motley crew of Muslims had burnt a copy of *The Satanic Verses* in Bradford, I felt drawn to answer those sensitive souls who had suggested that 'next they will be burning human beings'. 'What stuff and nonsense!' I wrote at the time. 'It is one of the most tedious aspects of the liberal mentality that it will always be looking for threats where threats there are none. In a few days, this humdrum affair will be as dead as the proverbial dodo.'

Though strictly speaking not absolutely and literally accurate, this prediction did echo the feelings of the British people at the time, and this, I modestly admit, is just one of my many talents as a popular columnist. Often, I will ask my friendly milkman what he thinks about a particular subject, and then I will write it verbatim in my column, taking pains to 'tip' him twenty-five pence the following Christmas.

A month later, the Ayatollah sentenced Mr Rushdie to death. This, I felt, was the time to come out in the strongest possible terms in favour of the ancient English tradition of Free Speech. Perusing that week's column, I see that I did not beat about the bush. 'Mr Rushdie cannot be said to be wholly English, or even British. But this is not to say that he should not be allowed to write what he wants as long as it does not upset anyone,' I began, adding, 'In future, might I ask him to learn the value of those great English virtues of tact, discretion and compromise.'

At this point, the job of the regular columnist becomes somewhat trickier. Having come down so firmly against the Ayatollah, I found myself searching around for a new opinion with which to entertain my devoted readers. By the middle of March, I had returned to the subject. 'No champion of free speech has ever been more wholehearted than I,' my column of March 16th began, 'but is it not peculiarly arrogant of Mr 'Salman' Rushdie and his left-wing backers that they remain obsessed with his thoroughly tedious tome whilst the Thatcher Government they affect to despise is forced to piece together the disaster he has made of our happy relations with Iran?'

At the beginning of April, Arnold returned to the subject. 'I have ceaselessly spoken up for the right of Rushdie to say what he likes within reason,' I wrote, 'but now is the time to save the British taxpayer many millions of pounds by withdrawing all his police protection, thus allowing him to stand, for once, on his own two feet.'

Such forthright, indeed brave, opinions might jolt the average *Spectator* reader, who, if I judge the situation correctly, has little feel for the man (no doubt Asian or – dread word! – 'Afro-Carribean'!) on the Clapham Omnibus, should such noble contraptions still exist in these godless times, and who may well feel more at ease among the mealy-mouthed.

To the subject, Wallace, to the subject! I take up the reins in May of last year after 20,000 Moslems had marched against the author, many dressed in outlandish garb. Once again, I felt duty bound to pipe up for the British belief in Freedom of Speech. 'I come second to no man in my defence of Mr Rushdie's right to say what he wants within limits,' I began, 'but is it not profoundly nauseating that a man who has consistently maligned Her Majesty's Government should now come running, cap in hand, to beg for Her protection? However much one sympathises with the plight of this self-styled publicity seeker and arrogant troublemaker, the time must soon come when all just men find themselves chorusing, "Enough is enough! I disagree with what you say, and I would fight for your right to say it, but you have become a drain on the taxpayers!"'

Once again, Arnold had found a new 'twist' to an age-old epigram, and his trenchant column remained as fresh and provocative as ever.

The long hot summer of '89 was a troublesome time for the British columnist, with little to spark off his fiery opinions. After discussing the weather in my columns of August 5th ('How one longs for a welcome downpour!'), August 12th ('Three Cheers for the Great British Summer!'), August 19th ('Isn't it time we learnt to deal with our annual drought?') and August 26th ('Prosecute These Criminal Hose-Users!'), I felt that my readers might care for a change, so, on September 2nd, my Parker returned to Mr Rushdie.

'Now that our dusky fellow-countryman has had time to ponder the consequences of his mischief-making,' I began, 'is it not time for him to show the courage of his convictions by saying to one and all, "So sorry. My mistake. Let's withdraw it from the shelves and forget all about it. After all, it's only a book." Were he to show such courage, all true Britons would find cause to applaud him.'

Following a rigorously argued piece in December, defending Mr Rushdie's freedom and going on to argue for an extension of the blasphemy laws, I returned to the subject at the beginning of February. 'If Mr Rushdie were to take his courage in both hands and appear, say, in Bradford, flanked by all the chivalry of freedom-loving Britain, might not such an act of brave defiance do much more to impress the Muslims about the sanctity of free speech than any number of angry articles written in the press?' I wrote. Imagine my distress, then, when I discovered that Mr Terry Worsthorne had employed those very words when writing in the *Telegraph*! Great minds, forsooth . . . .

'Now is the time to save the British taxpayers many
millions of pounds.'

SIR ALFRED SHERMAN

The Jazz Years

*A*rnold here traces, with a few deft strokes of his pen, the
early growth of modern-day Conservatism to the smoky
haunts of New Orleans, all the while concentrating on the
rhythmic, magnetic, hip-hop character of the now largely
forgotten Sir Alfred Sherman.

W.A.

It was while Alfie 'Duke' Sherman, as he then was, was
playing back-up trombone for the late, great Satchmo
that he first grew to know and love the black man. And
it is because of this deep and abiding love that he is still
able to discriminate against him. To this very day,
when 'Sir Alfred', as he likes his closest friends to call
him, jives down All Saints Road, black men of every
shade and hue leap from the shadows to shake him by
the hand. 'The dude's got rhythm,' one of their fraternity explained to me a while ago. 'An' what's mo,' he
got *soul*.'

Among the Rastafarian community, he is treated
with a respect bordering on reverence. To them, he is
Haile Ras Sherman, a minor deity, upon whose head
flowers must be placed at all times. It is even said that
Mr Bob Marley had Sherman in mind when he penned
his immortal verse, 'Let's get together, and it'll be all
right.' As the Notting Hill Carnival approaches, the
time is fitting to pay tribute to this essentially lovable
figure.

Like Duke Ellington and Earl Scrugg before him, Sir Alfred Sherman has long been a source of inspiration to a rich variety of creative artists. It was while taking a youthful walk along a river-bank that he was first spotted by a young author called Kenneth Grahame, and the immortal figure of 'Toad of Toad Hall' was born. Professor Tolkien, too, found much to admire in the young Sir Alfred, and he often made it clear that, without him, there would have been no Hobbit. How comforting it is for parents the world over to know that, for as long as children flick through books, they will always be fingering the familiar, jovial figure of Sir Alf.

Not content to spend the rest of his life simply as a children's hero, Sir Alfred Sherman took off with his trombone to New Orleans, the home, as he puts it in his delightful autobiography, *Boogie Down with Alfie*, of 'hootin', tootin', red-hot jazz'. He was never to look back. As plain Al Sher, he was soon backing all the greats, among them Blind Boy Williams, Black Jack Malone and the then virtually unknown Perry 'Peregrine' Perry (dubbed 'The Worst Horn in Town').

Odd, I suppose, that so many of our leading right-wing polemicists should have learnt their craft in the smoky haunts of New Orleans. It was by no means unusual in those days to find oneself jamming in the early hours with, say, Mary Kenny on sax and Wailin' Paul Johnson on castanets.

Back in London, Sir Sher, as he now styled himself, founded the Dance Centre for Policy Studies, with the intention of combining right-wing Conservative thought with the Negro rhythm-and-blues, but in the end it was the Conservative thought which gained the upper hand. A shame, for Sir Sher was always a dab hand at the blues, and not, frankly, much of a thinker.

THE SPECTATOR

Doughty journal!

*T*hough few people read the Spectator, Wallace Arnold
has stuck by it through thick and thin. His weekly
'Afore Ye Go' affords a refuge of urbane wit and agreeable
small talk in a journal otherwise overburdened with the
waspish and the high-falutin'. Here, he pays generous tribute
to 160 years of this funny little magazine.

W.A.

Forget thee not, dear reader, that throughout all its
immensely distinguished 160 years, the *Spectator* has
commanded a fearsome reputation as, above all else, a
journal of *campaign*. For the *Spectator*, the future has
never been something which is bound to happen, come
what may. Far from it. Those who dwell in the future,
successive generations of correspondents have argued,
are constrained by the fallacy that the past has been and
gone.

As early as 1870, this journal was mounting forceful
campaigns against the motor car ('unfeasible and muddle-headed') and the telephone ('vulgar, disagreeable
and demonstrably impractical'). This sure-footed cam-
paigning did much to halt the forward march of those
two monstrous contraptions, and it is widely believed
that their use would be far more widespread in our own
day were it not for those siren calls of a century past.

Never for the *Spectator* the unthinking adoration of
things Foreign. The Edwardian era found the *Spectator*

taking up the cudgels against Foreign wine ('grapy, sly and ingratiating'), Foreign travel ('a brisk stroll along the sea-front at Eastbourne yields infinitely greater riches than a year spent muddling through the "treasures" of Italy') and Foreign languages ('unEnglish').

Nor would 'innovation', that old spine-chiller of a word, cut much ice with the deft pens employed by the *Spectator*. When, to their unabashed distress, the production of the motor car seemed unlikely to tail off, as they had confidently predicted, our correspondents switched their fire to the ruination of British roads. In particular, they deplored the notion that human beings could be restricted to driving only on one side or the other, preferring a *laissez-faire* policy whereby, should one espy, say, a view pleasing to the eye, one would be well within one's rights to drift over to the lane best-suited to its fuller perusal.

As 'innovations' gathered apace, so too did the *Spectator*'s robust condemnation. It looked askance at any novelty advertised by its perpetrators as a 'benefit for mankind'.

Fire extinguishers, the wireless, garden furniture, penicillin, paperbacks and the flushing lavatory have all, at one time or another, smarted from the wrath of the *Spectator*'s trenchant criticism. Similarly, the *Spectator* has never been fool enough to fall for the fashionable *bêtes noires* of the woolly-minded liberal fraternity, preferring to allot praise where praise is due. Thus we have praised the virtues of asbestos ('I would happily feed it to my babe-in-arms,' wrote one contributor), poison gas ('a rather agreeable velvety aroma') and full-scale nuclear war ('there is no doubt that it will put paid to a great many indifferent and overpriced restaurants').

In our own age, the *Spectator*'s more recent campaigns for the retention of the old counties and against joining the Common Market have made successive governments think again. Of course, few of these campaigns have, in any grim sense of the word, 'worked', but then it has never been the business of a civilised journal to interfere with elected governments.

GENERAL ALFREDO STROESSNER

A literary reminiscence of the pen-pusher from Paraguay

It has been said of Wallace Arnold that he has supped, at one time or another, with anyone of any significance. But, as this dazzling exercise in biography demonstrates, sometimes a talent flowers in an area other than that in which it was first sown.

W.A.

Not the first South American president to go under and, I daresay, not the last; but Freddy Stroessner must surely be one of the few South American dictators in recent years to have combined a successful career in politics with a by no means unsuccessful career as an occasional essayist for the small magazines. It is for this reason, I would hazard a guess, that the editorial board of the *Spec* decided not to come down too hard on the old boy ('a remarkable man . . . he presided over a great expansion in Paraguay's prosperity . . .') when penning his retirement appraisal last week.

It was through his writing that I first came to know Freddy. As Michael Sheldon points out in his excellent new *Friends of Promise*, the 'Country Matters' column in *Horizon*, simply signed 'A.S', was a veritable goldmine of eagle–eyed observation from one who knew every butterfly in every albeit Paraguayan hedgerow. One week 'A.S.' would be informing the London literati how best to cook the wings of a butterfly, the next he would tell us how to flush out subversives hiding in hedgerows.

But as his military ambitions grew broader, so too did his literary ambitions. Once he had become a full general in the Paraguayan Army, Freddy made it crystal clear to the editors of the small London magazine – *Life and Letters*, *Time and Tide*, *Shake and Vac*, and so on – that he would no longer be confined to singing the praises of Mother Nature. No: he was determined to expand into literary appreciations and even critical reappraisals. Of course, the small editors had no choice but to cave in.

Well do I remember my first meeting with Freddy Stroessner. Through swathes of cigarette smoke and gales of literary laughter at the first anniversary party of *Tiny Wee*, that doyen of small magazines, I espied a severe-looking man reading a slim volume of Dylan Thomas, dressed in the full military regalia of the Paraguayan High Command. 'That, my dear,' said Cyril, noticing my interest, 'is Freddy Stroessner. Absolute poppet. *Very* Paraguayan, of course. Shy, too. Do have a word – he's just written a piece on the Leavises.'

Even at our first meeting, it was clear to me that Stroessner was a man in a hurry to conquer new territory. Did I know anyone on the *TLS*? Had I read his piece on the new Powell? Later, on the very same day that he became the new President of Paraguay, Freddy composed an excellent piece on the Brownings which he sent to the editor of the *New Statesman* with a covering letter detailing his plans to infiltrate the areas staked out by Connolly, Edmund Wilson and Joe Ackerley. A little too pushy for the London literary scene of the time, Stroessner's career never really got off the ground. But he will have earned himself a small footnote in the history of London literary life, and that in itself is no mean feat, methinks.

MR NORMAN TEBBIT

A life in music

A devoted opera lover, Arnold has often attended perform-
ances in the company of the highest in the land. Whether
writing on the subject of classical music, or on his other
overwhelming love – people – his prose always has the sweep
and flow of great opera. Here, he combines his two interests to
write a prose-poem describing his trip with Mr Norman
Tebbit to the Nelson Mandela Concert, held at Wembley to
celebrate the release from prison of the ANC leader.

W.A.

I am all for a little musical fun; indeed, in my days as a
Boy Scout I would always be the first to strike up a
chorus of 'Gin Gan Goolie' as the baked 'beans' were
lowered on to the smoking kindling. 'Gin Gan Goolie
Goolie Goolie Goolie Watcha,' I would bellow, the
smell of 'beans' wafting up my 'shorts', 'Gin Gan Goo,
Gin Gan Goo'. So let it never be said that Wallace
Arnold is a killjoy when it comes to the singsong.

But there are singsongs and there are singsongs. The
Monday before last, I found myself at Wembley Sta-
dium, my ears ringing from the incessant dirge of 'pop'
music thumping away. In front of me and behind, to
my left and to my right, young people, many of them
having ostentatiously removed their neck-ties before
arrival, cavorted and gyrated, twisting their bodies into
angles and positions more suited to the medical text-
book than to the public forum. 'Snogging' (dread

word!) appeared to be the order of the day, with couples treating each other in the open air with an intimacy more usually reserved for rubber dollies in the privacy of the bedchamber. Bodies rubbed against bodies in time to the jungly rhythms of the performers, unashamed affection running rife through both stalls and circle. That the young lassie in front of me pooh-poohed participation in the quiet rhumba I sought to initiate might be blamed on the radical feminist indoc-trination she no doubt received, courtesy the tax-payer. But what cannot be excused is the presence of the Leader of the Opposition at an event so tribal, so political and so irredeemably youthful.

I speak, of course, of the 'Nelson Mandela' concert, at which one's ears were blasted by a variety of per-formers, some of them as white as you or me, others less so. I went as a guest of Mr Norman Tebbit, who has long had an interest in the Latin-American rhythms of Mr James Last and his Orchestra, but whose princi-pal interest in the event was to ascertain for which side those attending were batting. He had also, as I under-stand it, strong hopes of borrowing the 'mike' from Mr Mandela for a few minutes to drum up support among the young there present for his 'Nips out' campaign, but alas to no avail.

Mr Tebbit had invited a wide variety of *Spectator* columnists to the event, wisely wishing to consolidate his directorship of this journal by buttering up the scriveners. Normally the most informed of men, he was under the impression that Mr Val Doonican would be 'topping the bill', and promised each of us that he had used his influence backstage to facilitate a rendition of 'Paddy McGinty's Goat', that perennial favourite.

Sadly, disappointment was the order of the day. Mr Doonican never appeared. Mr Mandela, a man for whom, imprisoned and silenced, I had the very greatest respect, chose to say little or nothing about keeping the

Chinky Chinaman at bay. The crowd seemed to be
batting for cloud-cuckoo land. And, throughout, the
diabolic grunts and groans of orgiastic mumbo-jumbo
drowned out my determined whistling of 'Gin Gan
Goolie Goolie Goolie Goolie Watcha, Gin Gan Goo,
Gin Gan Goo'.

MRS MARGARET THATCHER

Our friend in need

*A*rnold's close friendship with the Prime Minister is well chronicled on other pages. Whilst some commentators who once swore loyalty appeared somewhat mealy-mouthed in their devotion after Mrs Thatcher's popularity began to plummet after the introduction of the Poll Tax in spring 1990, Arnold refused to waver. This remarkable piece explains why.

W.A.

As one of the Prime Minister's most steadfastly loyal intimates, I have found the media (d.w.!) response to the difficulties faced by the Party peculiarly distasteful. The vast majority of Tories, myself included, remain wholly supportive of the achievements of this remarkable woman, quite regardless of the current media hubbub. Weathering the storm has long been the hallmark of the true Conservative, and we will not let the left-inspired machinations of Mr Brian Redhead *et al.* bulldoze us into throwing out our most precious asset willy-nilly.

Having said this, it must also be clear that many Tories, including myself, may come, during the full course of events, to consider the possibility that it is high time we got rid of this shrill female with her high-handed approach to the ordinary citizens of our land. Now is the time for all who have benefited from the revolution in British politics over the past eleven years to rally around our leader, to offer her our help and encouragement and to suggest that, over a decent period of a day or two, she should pack her bags and be gone.

I myself tried to warn the Party against the imposition of the Community Charge no less than three years ago. 'This is a long-needed reform for which the country is crying out,' I wrote, and it was only loyalty to the Party which prevented me from being more stinging in my criticism. Similarly, I warned a full eighteen months ago of the strides Labour was making towards electoral success. 'Kinnock's collection of misfits and mongrels is as dud today as it ever was,' I hinted in October '88, the savagery of my remarks tempered by a disinclination to praise.

Who, then, should we turn to? My own crisp oncer is on Michael, whom I have already contacted with a view to offering my services in his forthcoming campaign and thereafter. Though in reviewing his last book, *Forward with the Future* (1989), I made some small criticisms of his 'sloppy thinking, extreme personal vanity and haphazard hold on the truth', I have since come to respect him for his incisive mind, his integrity and his complete lack of airs. I have known him since his days as a window-dresser in the old Derry and Toms, where he was to acquire the skills that were later to stand him in good stead at Liverpool, and after that as Mr Christopher Trace's predecessor on the excellent *Blue Peter*. It was the sight of so many unemployed men and women in the 1950s that turned him into a lifelong Conservative, and I have now come firmly to believe that he is the man to lead Britain into a more caring era of Tory rule.

Nobody can take away the astounding achievements of Margaret Thatcher, and the fact that her later years were marred by extreme pigheadedness will, one feels

sure, do nothing to stem the flow of coppers we will
receive for a suitable leaving memento. But, until that
distant day, let us hear no more from the media of any
cock-and-bull 'leadership crisis'!!

UNCALLED FOR

A brief rebuff

In this abrupt diary item, Arnold exercised his 'right to reply' after a fashionable but ill-conceived film set out to drag his name through the dirt. Note that his celebrated sense of fun still holds strong, even in times of adversity.

W.A.

My name is often bandied about when one wordsmith partakes of snuff with another, but I must admit that I am unused to hearing it blasting loud and clear from the Big Screen. Though I barely met Miss Keeler during my frequent sojourns at Cliveden, the makers of a new motion picture called, if memory serves, *Sandal!* (misleading, as footwear plays little or no part in the proceedings) have seen fit to drag my reputation through the dirt by constant reference to 'leading society figures' implicated in the so-called sandal. They nowhere mention W. Arnold by name, courage not being high on their list of credentials, but when Miss Keeler says, 'The only man who ever made me truly happy in this whole extraordinary affair which led to the downfall of a Government is a well respected literary figure who is a frequent guest and confidant in the highest political circles', it takes no detective to divine at whom the finger points. But I have made it a rule never to pass comment on this sorry episode, and it is a rule I have no intention of breaking.

But for that episode (how unnecessary to bring up

'I have made it a rule never to pass comment on this sorry episode.'

the name of John Profumo) my memories of Cliveden are of civilised people from all walks of life hobnobbing with one another. On one lawn, the young Imelda Marcos might be sharing small talk with the First Lord of the Treasury, whilst on another Mr Frankie Vaughan would be getting to grips with the Suez Crisis with the then Quintin Hogg, and, on the Upper Terrace, Rab would be testing his mettle in a hand of gin rummy with Mr Norman Wisdom and two of the Beverley Sisters. Golden days indeed, but then Astor went ahead with his plans for building a swimming pool, against my repeated advice, and the allure of bathing togs was too much for some people to withstand. A sad end to a glorious summer.

THE VICTORIA AND ALBERT MUSEUM

A life in Art

*In this intriguing passage of autobiography, especially com-
missioned by the influential* Antique *magazine, Arnold
reveals the growth of his passion for the Arts, a passion which
culminated in his continued Trusteeship of the prestigious
Victoria and Albert Museum.*

W.A.

It must have been in the late Fifties or early Sixties
(dread decade!) when Mr Peter Rachman, a distinguished property magnate of the time, cornered me
in the snug bar of the Garrick in order to 'Sound me
out' as to the advisability of, as he put it, 'moving in on'
the Art market.

This, you should remember, was at a time when de
Chiricos were selling down the Portobello Road for 2/6
and the price of a ham sandwich, so it might fairly be
said that Rachman was something of a visionary. He
had, it emerged, met Sir Harold Acton on his holiday
somewhere out East, and Acton had advised him to
barge in double-quick on Art before every last Thomas, Richard and Harold discovered the cash to be had
from canvases. Over an agreeable claret, Rachman
looked me full-square in the eyes and implored me to
take up the post of his Personal Art Adviser. Heady
times indeed. Brandishing the Rachman (UK) Ltd Art
and Rent Enforcement Account, the figure of Wallace
Arnold soon became a familiar sight among the most

exclusive art dealers of the Bayswater Road. My ability to recite the first three Cantos of Dante's *Divina Commedia* off by heart, combined with a readiness to cross his ample palms with sufficient green 'uns, convinced Sir Bernard Berenson that the position of in-house Authenticator would be worthy of his by no means inconsiderable talents. By the end of the first year's trading, I had managed to pick up a variety of world masterpieces, and all for an average price of £7/10. Sir Bernard had loyally authenticated a magnificent Turner watercolour, believed to be the great artist's only painting of a dewy-eyed clown, a delightful Tintoretto entitled 'Just Good Friends!' of a lovable pooch and a canary sitting side by side in front of an electric fire, and a quite outstanding modern masterpiece by Pablo Picasso, believed to be the only extant example of his little-known Horses-On-Sand-By-Sunset Period. Rachman was delighted; Sir Bernard was well remunerated; and in no time at all Wallace Arnold had secured himself an enviable position at the very forefront of London's burgeoning Art market.

It must have been shortly after Rachman found himself interned at Her Majesty's Pleasure that I first received a call from Nik Ceausescu, who, as newly-appointed President of Romania, found himself confronted by the onerous responsibility of decorating his new Palace. Could I, he wondered, purchase the very finest of *objets d'art* on offer in Europe for him and his lady wife, and, while I was about it, could I pick up an acceptable gold-plated jacuzzi and an Executive Bar-B-Q from the celebrated Harrods Department Store in Knightsbridge?

I set about my new task with aplomb, and within a month I had shipped over to Romania over fifty vast and dazzling sunsets, all in brilliant golds and oranges, many of them attributable to Vermeer. Nik and Elena were delighted and, settling their by no means insubstantial bill with commendable alacrity, ordered up a host of further Old Masters, among them Giotto's 'Blue Lady' and an early Caravaggio, 'Tennis Girl with Bare Bottom'. By now, the mere mention of the name of Wallace Arnold drew sighs of envy from all the most prestigious art dealers in Europe.

The decade of the Eighties has seen the rise of the international businessman as sophisticated art connoisseur, and Wallace Arnold Fine Arts Inc. has risen to the challenge, attributing and acquiring. Only the other month, the familiar, commanding tones of Mr Alan Bond, Antipodean financial supremo, came on the blower.

'Wallace,' he said, 'Wallace, would you know a painter called Iris?'

'Iris? Iris?' I replied. 'Now there you have me, Alan. But I'm sure I can find one.'

'The wife's mad on her stuff. Seems that she's painted a picture of a Dutchman by the name of Van Gogh. So I'd like you to get me Iris's Van Gogh when it comes up. Have a word with Grey Gary at Sotheby's about when to stick your mit in the air, are you with me?'

Needless to say, Grey Gary is just one of my many contacts in the senior echelons of the London Art World, and others include Sir Roy Strong and leading patron Bubbles Lady Rothermere. Now that I am a Trustee of the Victoria and Albert Museum, I find myself more than ever determined to bring Art kicking and screaming into the real world, away from the squalid little artists' studios of folklore and into the boardrooms of those who shape our destinies. I am thus delighted to be able to employ the pages of *Antique* magazine in order to announce our First Annual Prize for Contemporary Portraiture, kindly sponsored by the Pergamon Press in association with Mirror Group Newspapers. The subject is EITHER *Still Life with Mr*

Robert Maxwell OR *Figure of Mr Robert Maxwell in Landscape*, prizes will be awarded for beauty, tact and improvement, and all finalists will be on display in a special exhibition in the newly opened Birds Eye Juicy Cod Fries in Crispy Batter Extension. As one art-lover to many others, I salute all these valiant efforts to increase the input of money to artists, and vice versa.

MY VISION OF A CLASSLESS SOCIETY

Let's hear no more of all this 'class' nonsense!

Reviewing a jocular Christmas volume, The Book of Total Snobbery *by Lynne and Graham Jones, Arnold seizes the opportunity to argue on behalf of those less well-born than himself, and, in so doing, reveals the humble origins of many of those whose present-day sophistication we take for granted.*

W.A.

No snob, I, but then one rarely encounters snobbery in those who come from what used to be called a 'good background'. Snobbery exists to a far greater extent among those upon whom breeding, in her wisdom, has not seen fit to smile.

The well-bred are invariably only too happy to open their doors to every Tom, Dick or Harold. 'Where the milkman whistles, there whistleth I' has long been the motto *chez* Arnold, and I oft find myself wishing tradesmen and artesans a cheery good morrow before closing the door behind them. Nor have I ever held back from forming a friendship with a man (or woman!) simply because he (or she!) is not what one might call 'top drawer'. Indeed, many of my closest literary and political friendships are with those who, through sheer dint of perseverance, have managed to cover the traces of their humble origins.

Take, for example, my dear friend Mr 'Peregrine' Worsthorne, forsooth. Few would now guess that this elegant sophisticated man-about-town was originally a plumber's mate from Catford. As luck would have it, in 1948 Terry Worst, as he was then, won third prize in a 'Spot the Football' competition organised by *Plunger*, the official organ of the Federation of Chartered Plumbers. His reward – dinner for one at London's Savoy Hotel, with all the trimmings – transported him into the thick of a world he had encountered previously only in his wildest dreams. Still in his familiar blue plumber's overalls – albeit supplemented with a borrowed neck-tie of garish blue – Terry Worsthorne stared, open-mouthed and eyes agog, at the assembled big-wigs who were seated at the tables around him. To his left, the then Raine McCorquodale was laughing elegantly at the risqué 'knock-knock' jokes of Sir Bernard and Lady Docker, who were hosting a fondue-dip for top American entertainer Mr Danny Kaye. To his right, Cecil Beaton exchanged waspish anecdotes concerning the then Queen with Mr Hardy Amies. Behind him, George Weidenfeld, dapper in white tie and tails, spooned extra gravy on to a plate for a famished customer, for these were his days as a waiter, some little while before he rose to become one of London's premier publishers.

The rest of the story is, as they say, history. Young Worst changed his Christian name from Terry to Teregrine and then finally to Peregrine, exchanged his plumber's overalls for a smart two-piece suit (often, alas, erroneously wearing the jacket back-to-front in the early months) and successfully altered his distinctive Catford twang through careful study of the early cinematic triumphs of Mr Rex Harrison. He then set out to acquire a distinguished and varied set of opinions, largely from car boot sales, and, within twenty years, he had carved himself a niche as our foremost thinker and man-of-letters, as happy to break bread with Princess Michael of Kent as to send a 'nice cuppa' out to a visiting car mechanic.

Others of my closest friends have triumphed over similar adversities. Sir Roy Strong originally enjoyed no small success as 'Strong Rosamund', a female mud wrestler, until one night an ill-fitting swimsuit blew his guise and he found himself booed out of the ring. The very next morning, he donned his familiar specs-nose-and-whiskers novelty mask and decided, there and then, to move full tilt into the glamorous world of museum curatorship, helped in his quest by Sir Kenneth Clark, an old colleague from his days as a soft-drinks-and-beverages steward on the old Great Eastern Line. Still others, whom many outsiders probably regard as top drawer, have admitted to me in private something of their lowly origins. Few would realise, for instance, that my old quaffing-partner Kenneth Rose was the original bass player in the world-famous James Last Orchestra, and that it is his nimble finger-work that is to be heard on 'Non-Stop Party-A-Go-Go Volume One', nor that Mrs Betty Kenward, now the charming 'Jennifer' of *Jennifer's Diary*, is the great aunt of Mr Jeremy Beadle, host of TV's *Beadle's About*. Similarly, Prince Philip's half-brother Steve is the manager of Mr Rolf Harris. British society in the 20th century has been very much more fluid (dread word!) than its enemies on the hard left would suggest.

And so to the mirthsome tome under scrutiny. It is packed full of marvellous *aperçus* which merit ten-out-of-ten on the famous Arnold chucklometer(!), including this positive gem from Lynne and Graham's introduction: 'We have to admit to a little home truth ourselves: no one who was NOT at least in part a snob could have penned this high-hatted tome.'

Priceless! As a veteran of the ticklish tome – *It's a Dog's Life – Wallace Arnold on the Lighter Side of Petulant Pooches* (Weidenfeld 1977); *The Unfairer Sex – Wallace*

Arnold on Women (Robson Books, 1981), *Boom! Boom! The Wit and Wisdom of Wallace Arnold* (Pavilion Books, 1983) etc., etc. – I take my hat off to Lynne and Graham for coming up with a splendidly humorous slim vol, full of hilarious questions such as 'So what is the new snobbery? Basically, it's dropping names not aitches; unsuitable friends, not clangers.' Bliss! Indeed, such verbal felicity combined with a most uncanny social omniscience suggests to the eagle eye of Arnold that 'Lynne and Graham Jones' might very well be the latest pseudonym for no less a couple than the Duke and Duchess of York, though breathe not a word to Lilibet.

THE WEIDENFELD TRILOGY

Of parties, publishing, princesses and pontiffs!

*T*he larger-than-life figure of publisher and man-about-town Lord Weidenfeld wafts through all the writings of Wallace Arnold like the scent of flowers on a spring morning. Occasionally, however, Arnold will place Weidenfeld in the forefront, devoting an entire pen-portrait to capturing the essence of the man. In this trilogy of pieces, culled from years of friendship, Arnold recalls with characteristic affection Weidenfeld's penchant for typographical errors, his meeting with the Pope and, finally, his short-lived marriage to Barbara Skelton, who was to write about their tempestuous relationship in her second volume of autobiography, Weep No More.

W.A.

(1)

I see that Duff Hart-Davis has seen fit to criticise My Lord Weidenfeld for the poor standards of editing rife in his esteemed company. Never one to miss a leg-pull, I would humorously venture that Duff is claiming that Weidenfeld is himself Duff. (Pardon my pun! I couldn't resist the light-hearted jest!)

Far be it from me to take sides. George and I go back goodness knows how long, and I am a regular ornament at his Chelsea *soirées*, swapping badinage and intrigue with the Great and the Good, while My Lordship surveys the assembly with eagle eye. 'Arianna, my

'Few would now guess that this elegant man-about-town was originally a plumber's mate from Catford.'

dear,' he bellowed a few evenings ago, and I became gradually aware that he had mistaken me for Miss (Ms!) Stassinopoulos-Huffington, 'you must write us a book – I *insist*.' I swiftly realised the reason for his mistake. A busy man, whose time is money, he recently employed a time-and-motion specialist to advise him on how to get the most out of his parties. After taking tape-measure, compasses and pocket calculator – albeit discreetly – to the guests in question, the specialist advised My Lordship that he should dramatically streamline all social encounters, never talking to one person without looking at another, never looking at one person without talking to another. Alas, the other evening was something of a 'try out' for this new method, and this explained the case of mistaken identity; I am reliably informed that My Lordship has now perfected his technique, and is quite able to negotiate a deal with, say, the good Dr Owen, while nodding appreciatively at every word that floats from the tongue of Bubbles Rothermere.

Sharp as ever, I could not help noticing that a number of what I believe are known in the publishing trade as 'literals' – plain old mistakes to you and I, forsooth! – were creeping into Lord Weidenfeld's conversation. 'Margaret, my dear, I feel sure there is a cook in you,' he chanced to say to the Duchess of Argyll the other day. Needless to say, the Duchess looked suitably horrified. 'A cook in me?' she bellowed, quite aghast. 'I have never been so insulted,' and, with that, she stormed away. 'But I only wanted her to wipe a book for us,' explained a forlorn George. Turning to Lady Elizabeth Anson for consolation, he purred, 'Elizabeth, darling, you really know how to make a tarty swing – you must write us a book.' Alas, Liz, too, took it the wrong way, slamming the door behind her.

'Delighted to meet you,' he said, upon being presented to Daniel Ortega at the Pinters', 'How do you poo?' Happily, the interpreter received the sack. All went well for George until the liqueurs, when he turned to Ortega and said, 'Daniel, my dear, I know you have a sock in you. You must let us publish it.' Alas, the Nicaraguan leader took him at his word, and a selection of Ortega's used socks appears in this autumn's Weidenfeld catalogue.

★ ★ ★

(II)

And many happy returns of the day to my old quaffing-partner, George Weidenfeld, seventy years young on Wednesday. To his many close friends and admirers – none more prominent than I – he is so very much more than just a grotesquely fat social climber, and it is to a portrait of this fascinating, enigmatic character that I turn my pen this week.

Picture, if you will, the scene: the low, strangely mournful Italian sun allows itself a final flicker as it sets behind the rooftop at Castel Gandolfo this summer. Pope John Paul II, in sparkling form, turns to the man on his right and asks him whom they can expect from England for the weekend. The man on the Pope's right – but why beat about the bush, for it is indeed I, Wallace Arnold – announces the imminent arrival of Lord Weidenfeld.

'Wei-Den-Feld' repeats His Holiness in his characteristic Polish burr, 'Wei-Den-Feld. A name I do not recognise, my dear Wally. Please explain.'

'Oh, George is the most *tremendous* fun, Your Holiness. Knows everyone. David Steel, Arianna Stassinopoulos, Princess Michael, Dickie Henderson. The lot. Loves a chinwag with the mighty. Simply cock-a-hoop about meeting Your Holiness, f'r'instance. You'll *love* him.'

'Wei-Den-Feld' repeats the Pope before continuing

to flick through the pages of an old copy of *Hello!* magazine.

George arrived promptly at six, overnight bag and autumn catalogue in hand. 'Delighted, delighted,' he purred upon being presented to the Pope. He then passed Il Papa the Weidenfeld autumn catalogue. 'For you, Your Holiness – absolutely free and without charge,' he explained. 'And I would ask you to tick up to six selections. Once you have made your choice at the unbelievable knockdown price of only £4.99 for any six, you are committed only to purchasing three recommended books over the course of the first year – money back if not delighted.'

This delightful vignette demonstrates, I think, the charming, virtually seamless way in which George likes to mix business with pleasure, linking Princes and Potentates to the illustrious name of Weidenfeld through the personal contact of the nod and the wink. The weekend conference at Castel Gandolfo concerned, of course, the great political, social and religious issues of the time – needless to say Arnold held forth, as per usual – but George lost no time in applying his magnetic charm to the Pope. 'You must write something for us, I *insist*,' he said, drawing the Pope to one side during a coffee-break. 'Tell me, what are your interests: gardening, for instance. You could do us a book on gardening. Anyway, here is my personal phone number. Ring me and we'll discuss it. Marvellous. Marvellous. A book on gardening it is, then.'

Sure enough, the Pope is now regularly to be seen at George's famous *soirées*, and his first book, *The Pope on Petunias*, is pencilled in for spring '91. We should all of us take this opportunity to salute a man who has given so much to English letters, whose books loom far larger than their numerous printing errors, and whose name is synonymous with quilaty.

★　　★　　★

(III)

My poor old friend and quaffing-partner George Weidenfeld has been the victim of merciless ribbing from
yours truly over the past week or two, I regret to say. 'I
say, George,' I quipped as he whistled to his butler to
plunge into the pantry for another string of chipolatas,
'I trust that there are no Skeltons [*sic*] in that
cupboard!!!'

Needless to say, the aforesaid jest went down like the
proverbial lead balloon. A quick-witted (if wide-
girthed!) man, George had apprehended my pun within
seconds. Let me explain: by skilful word-play, I had
rearranged the old English phrase, 'A skeleton in the
cupboard', so that it ran 'A Skelton in the cupboard',
the 'Skelton' in question being Miss (Ms!) Barbara
Skelton, who was once married to George, and is now
amusing the world of letters with pithy descriptions of
their none-too-jolly union. Small wonder, then, that
when I intoned, 'I trust that there are no Skeltons [*sic*] in
that cupboard!!!' George threw what I believe is known
as a 'wobbly'!!

Wicked punster I may be, but, like many very funny
men, I also have a heart. I could see that George was
upset, for he began to spoon scrambled eggs into his
mouth at high speed. 'She said I was a social climber!'
he spluttered. 'Anyone will tell you I'm not! Ask
Princess Michael of Kent! Ask Princess Margaret! Ask
two Popes, four crowned Princes, five Prime Ministers
and no fewer than twelve heads of State – go on, just
ask them!'

I remember well that short-lived marriage. The two
of them lived entirely separate lives. George, a starry-
eyed young man with aspirations, even then, towards
assisting this great democracy from a bench of his own

in the House of Lords, would spend his days in napkin-folding classes, his evenings studying flower arrangement and the art of conversation. Meanwhile, Barbara continued to attract the attention of the *haut monde* of London in the Fifties: at one moment, Ken Tynan would be whisking her off to an avant-garde milk bar, and the next moment a figure such as Arthur Askey would be performing his 'Buzzy Bee' routine in the privacy of her bedroom. Harold Macmillan, Gerald Hamilton, Douglas Fairbanks Jr, Cecil Beaton, Lonnie Donegan, Viscount Montgomery, Group Captain Peter Townsend and Lord Rockingham's XI all passed through her life at one time or another. Needless to say, this constant flow of visitors constituted a great distraction for George, who was, at the time, mid-way through his Advanced Diploma in Social Poise and Small-Talk. One night, the sound of 'Buzz, Buzz, Buzz, Buzzy Bee' emanating through their thin walls proved too much for George as he struggled to fold a paper napkin into a lifelike swan, and the marriage came to an abrupt end. A sorry business, and I now feel saddened that it ever afforded me cause for mirth.

WOMEN

Being something of a love-letter!

Invited by Punch *magazine to review a new book by Shere Hite and Kate Colleran called* Good Guys, Bad Guys and Other Lovers – Every woman's guide to relationships, *Arnold gives way to his emotions and takes the opportunity to offer readers a valuable insight into his own dealings with the species he once memorably referred to as 'The Unfairer Sex!'*

W.A.

I have long had something of a *penchant* for birds of the unfeathered variety(!), and I rather think that the feelings are reciprocated. Where would we be without women, those essentially cuddlesome creatures, many of whom are by no means unadept with oven glove and drying-up cloth? This is the main gist of this stimulating (Pardon my French!) and fascinating work, penned, as it is, by two easy-on-the-eye blue-stockings.

It is an open secret that I made something of a name for myself as a 'woman watcher' or 'female fancier' in the early Seventies with my famous series of articles for *Punch* – then at the height of its Tickle Quotient under the twinkling eye of Bill Davies – which went out under the title 'Wallace's Wondrous Women', with illustrations by the redoubtable Barry Appleby. This series was, in its way, something of a humorous trailblazer, and is still spoken of in hushed tones whene'er two mirth-makers meet. In 1976, you will remember, the series was turned into a two-part special for Radio 2's Comedy Half-Hour starring my old mate and quaffing-partner Terry Scott, with 'girly voices' by Uncle Roy Hudd, and later that same year Leslie Frewin published that gem of a stocking-filler, *Watch Out, Women – Wallace is About!*, with an introduction by HRH Prince Philip, who, I might add, can tell his fillies from his geldings, if you'll excuse the analogy, Your Highness!!!

In his splendid introduction, HRH Prince Philip, who, let's face it, has seen a thing or two, opined that 'Women can be demanding, tiresome, over-spending, nagging, and sometimes just downright impossible, but where would we fellows be without that splendid skirted species???!!!' I try to keep this right royal aphorism in my mind whenever the Unfairer Sex(!) has conspired to drive me round the proverbial bend, and I might add that it works mighty well, me hearties. While escorting my latest comely lovely to a candlelit dinner at a local *trattoria*, I take especial care to maintain my conversation on what I call a 'Level Fit for the Female Lughole', keeping off anything too intellectual, political or abstract, veering rather more towards talk of frocks, film stars and assorted fripperies, but still, I find, it is by no means hard to 'put one's foot in it', and then Prince Philip is one's only succour.

Let me share an example with you. Having known her Dad from way back, I felt I had reasonable excuse to ask Miss (Ms!) Germaine Greer out for a little *diner à deux* at Mario's, a by no means inexpensive little place, a stone's throw from my 'bachelor penthouse'. Mario himself could not have been more engaging, directing us to a quiet table in the corner. 'Meeester Arnold,' said Mario, 'You always choose the most beeooodiful girls!' With this compliment he winked at Miss Greer, and, passing me the wine-list, moved on.

'Brute,' said Miss Greer, her teeth clenched.

'Close,' I replied, 'but Eau Sauvage, actually. Now, stop worrying that pretty little head and pick yourself something to eat. Doubtless you'll need help with translation – If so, Arnold at your service, ha ha!'

Dinner went swimmingly. Steering well clear of 'heady' subjects, I entertained Miss Greer with some of the finest anecdotes from the Life and Times of Wallace Arnold, including my meeting in a lift with Beaver-brook himself, saving the day at the '87 General Election and subsequent compliments from Mrs T., Arnold on so-called 'progressive' art, and contradiction in terms thereof(!), holidaying with Sir Harold Acton in *Firenze*, my days as a stalwart of the *Punch* lunch (most estimable of repasts!), my invitation as *Jester Extraordinaire* to Prince Andrew's stag night, and finally, over coffee and liqueurs, a rendition of my escapades of an amatory nature with some of the most bubbly young lovelies of the day.

Chuckling wholeheartedly at such delicious reveries, it was not until the bill (the damage!) arrived, and I was half-way through insisting that I pay at least some of it, that I noticed that Miss Greer was nowhere to be seen. Mario later confessed that he had spotted la Greer exiting from his *ristorante* midway through her prawn cocktail. Such were the shadows cast by candlelight, combined with my fierce enjoyment of my trips down memory lane, that I had quite simply forgotten to check that the 'little lady' was still in attendance! Nevertheless, a hugely entertaining evening, and, as Mario explained with typical earthiness, 'Women! They just no listen!'

All of which brings me to the book in hand. The two lovely lasses who put pen to paper share with me a love of that most entrancing of meals, the Great British Picnic. 'Fighting the stereotypes is no picnic,' they quip at one stage, 'The "I am right and you are wrong" style during a fight is no picnic!' they hoot at one another.

Alas, they nowhere tell us what *is* a picnic. Doubtless they will let us know in a second volume. Personally, I can't be doing without scotch eggs and a well-chilled *Chablis*, but I am prepared to concede that these bountiful beauties have ideas of their own. Which is as it should be, in this day and age, methinks.

HRH THE DUCHESS OF YORK

Marvellous memories of a Royal christening

*P*rompted by the publication of Budgie the Little Helicopter, *the widely acclaimed first book by the Duchess of
York, Arnold takes a trip down memory lane, painting an
enchanting word-picture of the christening of Princess Beatrice
and recalling his first meeting with his very dear friend, the
authoress. Note the appearance, also, of the Duke of Edinburgh, who again lets his temper get the better of him in a
manner that calls to mind his unfortunate luncheon with Mr
Andy Warhol, described in full a few pages back.*

W.A.

I well remember the christening of Baby Beetroot, as
her mother, the author of this delightful tome, likes to
call her. We, the godparents, had gathered in St
George's Chapel and were 'talking among ourselves'.
On my left was the popular singer and all-round family
entertainer Mr Des O'Connor, to my right that veritable *doyen* of magicians, Mr Paul Daniels.

As parents, relations and godparents foregathered
around the font, I made every attempt to 'soak in' all
that I saw, ready to record the scene for posterity in my
celebrated commonplace book. This was, indeed, history in the making, and Wallace Arnold was its dutiful –
and greatly privileged – chronicler.

★   ★   ★

'"Budgie" continued the Duchess, "is a naughty little helicopter with a great big tummy".'

The reader might well be asking whether it was my friendship with the Duke's family or the Duchess's that found Arnold standing in St George's Chapel that sunny morn. Both, to be frank. My friendship with Major Ronnie 'Ron' Ferguson goes back many years to the time when he was a bookie's stringer working the Doncaster circuit. I had been put in touch by a mutual contact who was a big noise in the Respray business. By the cut of his tweed, I always suspected that Honest Ron would go far, and I was not in the least surprised when I heard that my old quaffing-partner the Duke of Edinburgh had engineered him a position as Keeper of the Queen's Horses.

I had, of course, been pals with the Duke ever since I had been privileged to help him put his thoughts and general philosophy of life on paper in his two tomes, *Pulling Your Finger Out: Essays by HRH The Duke of Edinburgh* (1973) and *Backs to the Grindstone: Further Essays by HRH The Duke of Edinburgh* (1979). He had repaid my efforts by writing brief but witty forewords to four of my celebrated *Lighter Side of . . .* series, notably *Wallace Arnold on the Lighter Side of Motoring!* and *Wallace Arnold on the Lighter Side of Home Improvements!* Needless to say, I was overjoyed when these two old pals – the Duke and 'Major' Ron, as he now was – struck up some sort of business arrangement together. To see the 'Major' happy as Larry, resplendent in a spanking new set of tweeds, as he hobnobbed on the polo lawn with big-wigs of the calibre of Nigel Havers, Princess Michael and Jackie Stewart, did much to gladden the old heart.

It was not until the early 1980s – '83 or '84, I should imagine – that 'Major' Ron's comely young daughter, known as 'Fergie', first caught my eye. At the time, I was in the habit of attending West End clubs which catered exclusively to the needs of Captains of Industry and leading figures in the worlds of politics and the arts.

Open until way into the morning, these thoroughly respectable establishments would offer companionship – of the female variety(!) – to gentlemen who had undergone a busy day putting this great country of ours back on its feet once more.

Ron was in the habit of leading me by the proverbial nose to these perfectly above-board twenty-four-hour leisure emporia. On the night in question, we paid our tuppence ha'penny worth to enter a spanking new (or vice versa – I jest!) club which rejoiced in the name of the Tomcat, I know not why.

As one adjusted one's eyes to the deep, red basement light, one began to discern a bevy of luscious lovelies in little more than their birthday suits, each one of 'em making a beeline for 'Major' Ron and yours truly. Needless to say, we did little to impede their progress(!) and, in the twinkling of an eyelid, Ron was on that dance-floor waltzing to the strains of the latest platter by Mr Demis Roussos, a young dolly-bird of oriental hue draped about his person. Meanwhile, Arnold's eye had been taken by a strapping young hussy in the corner, busy telling 'knock knock' jokes to a party of Brazilian businessmen fresh from the Ideal Home Exhibition. Our eyes met, I blew her the famous Arnold kiss, and, before Mr Roussos had reached his heart-rending finale, the two of us were sharing a chuckle or two over a bottle of non-vintage champagne.

Her name was, she said, Esmerelda. 'Lovely name,' said I. 'Are you new to London?' she asked. 'Far from it,' said I, 'I know London intimately. Indeed, much of my column in that estimable journal, the *Spectator*, concerns my perambulations through this great capital. Do you read the *Spectator* at all?'

The poor love looked a mite perplexed. 'Sounds naughty!' she giggled, adding, 'Ooh, don't these bubbles get up your nose, know what I mean?'

Our conversation continued in such animation while

I explained to her the various delights of the *Spectator* – Mr Paul Johnson's sturdy yet iconoclastic 'think pieces', Mr Terry Worsthorne's impish diaries, Mr Ron Waugh's mirthful (if occasionally hurtful) merrymaking, and so on. 'I bet it's the pictures YOU go for, though, you naughty little boy!' she replied, but I did my level best to explain to her that the quality of prose was of paramount interest, though the illustrations were, admittedly, often pertinent and of high quality.

'But tell me about yourself, my dear,' I asked her, for I am very much a 'people person', but, alas, the crooner had completed his caterwauling, and 'Major' Ron was bounding over to us, Oriental lovely in tandem. Oddly enough, when he set his eyes on my own delightful companion, his face turned from pink to mauve and then to what can only be described as a livid purple.

'Sarah!' exclaimed Ron, quite out of the blue.

'Daddy!' exclaimed Esmerelda.

Frankly, I don't know who looked the more surprised. But, to cut a long story short, the tale ended happily enough, for, before the end of the evening, Her Majesty the Queen's second son, HRH Prince Andrew, having called into the Tomcat for a quick nightcap, had been quite taken with Esmerelda (née Sarah). Small world, small world. Esmerelda has since become the Duchess of York. Ron, I need hardly add, was over the proverbial moon, and I should think so too.

★ ★ ★

Needless to say, when the question of godparents arose, the name of Wallace Arnold was the first to dance upon their young lips. The other godparents were, in alphabetical order, Mr Paul Daniels, Miss Anne Diamond, Mrs Andrew Lloyd-Webber, Mr Desmond O'-Connor and, to offer spiritual guidance, Miss Claire Rayner. Rumour had it that Prince Andrew, having met and liked Mr Ronald 'Ronnie' Biggs while on a naval exercise in Brazil, had submitted his name as a godparent, only to have it turned down by the Queen.

And so let us return to the font, around which the above-mentioned distinguished personages had gathered. As the strains of 'Amazing Grace', sung 'live' by Mr Rod Stewart, died down, we were all encouraged by the Dean of Windsor to bend our heads in preparation for the first reading. 'I trust it will be from the Authorised Version,' I whispered to a heavily veiled Miss Rayner. 'None of this Good News nonsense, pshaw!'

But the reading was many miles removed from the Bible of any colour or complexion. Instead, the Duchess of York, dressed delightfully in a lime green knee-length tunic, sat on the side of the font. 'I thought that this would be a suitable time,' she said, 'to introduce you to my latest creation, "Budgie the Little Helicopter".'

'Ahh! Lovely!' whispered Mr O'Connor in the Arnold earhole.

'Budgie,' continued the Duchess, 'is a naughty little helicopter with a great big tummy – and he gets up to all kinds of mischief!!!'

'The first story I'd like to read you is called "Budgie the Helicopter Gets All in a Flutter!" and I'd like you all to join in whenever Budgie goes "Broom! Broom! Broom!" okay, gang?'

My eyes darted across to my old friend Prince Philip, whose right foot was tapping the Chapel floor with increasing rapidity while the vein in his neck grew ever more prominent.

'It was a hot, hot day,' began the Duchess, 'one of the hottest days anyone could remember. "Golly", thought Budgie the Little Helicopter, "This is a very hot day indeed. Talk about hot! I'm very, very hot!"

"Phew, am I hot!" said Budgie, "Why, I must be the

hottest little helicopter in the whole of the land, that's how hot I am!" Poor Budgie was so so very very hot, he even thought of changing his name to Hottie!!!'

Beside me, Mr Des O'Connor emitted a high-spirited giggle. 'Lovely joke, lovely,' he said under his breath while the Duchess continued with her tale.

Grabbing a chance to cast my eyes over the company assembled around said font, I noticed that 'Major' Ron, wearing a specs-nose-and-moustache 'novelty' mask to avoid the unwelcome attentions of the seedier end of the press, appeared to be enjoying the tale immensely, and so too were the vast majority of the celebrity godparents, but the same could not be said, alas, for Prince Philip, and HRH the Queen was pursing and re-pursing her lips in swift succession.

'My goodness, what a hot, hot day it was. But Budgie was a brave little helicopter and he wasn't going to sit around all day just because it was hot, oh, no. So he started his motor whirring – Broom, Broom, Broom – '

At this juncture, Miss Claire Rayner, who had been primed beforehand, led the congregation in a spirited chorus of 'BROOM, BROOM, BROOM, BROOM, BROOM, BROOM', with 'Major' Ron adding the necessary husky quality from his position at the back.

'Broom, Broom, Broom,' exclaimed the Duchess once more.

'BROOM, BROOM, BROOM,' went the rest of us.

'STOP IT! STOP IT! STOP IT AT ONCE, I SAY!' It was Prince Philip, red-faced and spitting with anger, screaming at the top of his voice.

'Oh-oh' said the Duchess, 'Someone's thrown a wobbly.'

* * *

Suffice it to say that we never did get to discover how Budgie the Little Helicopter managed to overcome the heat problem of that hot, hot day. But I rather suspect that it was the enforced curtailment of her readings from the 'Budgie' books at Baby Beetroot's christening that persuaded the Duchess to present them before the jury of a wider public. The great British public, I am glad to say, has given the opening tome a 'right royal thumbs up', to use the Duchess's phrase, and a further twenty volumes are planned for publication over the course of the next three years. The day I first heard them recited will remain long in my mind. Memories, as Mr O'Connor used to sing so plaintively, woah, woah, woah, Memories . . . .

OF ZIPS, MATES AND FAXES

Dread words, the lot of 'em!

*A common thread linking all Arnold's political and liter-
ary essays is an unremitting suspicion of Things
Modern. In this marvellously iconoclastic diatribe against the
new words that have entered the English language, he takes
unabashed delight in popping some of the great affectations of
our age.*

W.A.

Words, words, words. They hold a seemingly endless
fascination for one. By removing one letter from even
the most humdrum word, then replacing it with
another, one can entirely alter its meaning. Take the
word 'Terry', as in my old chum 'Terry Worsthorne'
f'r'instance: Ferry Worsthorne would mean something
quite different, so too would Merry Worsthorne, and I
would hazard that, were his admirable leading articles
to be signed 'Cherry Worsthorne', much of their estimable *gravitas* would leap 'out the window', as it were.

My pen alighteth on this particular theme under the
influence of last week's admirable Diary item by the
aforesaid Cherry(!) concerning the word 'naff' and
what on earth it means. On that one, frankly, W.
Arnold drew a blank: never 'eard of it, guv, as my
under-tailor might exclaim in a moment of bamboozle-
ment! But other new words strike one as equally
baffling.

'Fax' is just one example. 'Shall I "fax" it to you?'

'Do you have a "fax"?' 'What's your "fax" number?' I am asked constantly at 'with-it' parties these days. To be honest, I rather suspect that 'Fax' is a particularly sinister piece of homosexual jargon, and, when asked a question along these lines, I have made it a firm rule to take a sharp turn on the heels without so much as a backward glance at the offender.

And what, one might ask, is, or are, A 'wok'? Some new-fangled guru, no doubt. Enthusiastic women (of both sexes!!) are often saying to me, 'Wallace, I swear by my wok.' The notion of a tea-shirt I also find troubling. No one could have a healthier respect than I for afternoon tea ('one lump, please, matron!'), but it seems to be taking decorum a little too far for the young of today to dress especially for it. Mind you, there is, I have noticed, a great upsurge of interest in the vener-able institution of afternoon tea amongst our youthful friends. My nephew Rex is often to be seen slouching off for a 'Jam Session' with his 'Mates' (a type of condom).

What is one to make of it all? Certainly, I would hesitate before spooning my Strawberry Conserve from such a container, but perhaps I'm just an old 'square' ('a new word meaning old-fashioned'). Far be it from me to steal the thunder from my old mate Jaspistos (a pseudonym, surely) but I wonder how many readers can place a meaning to the following new words: 'Hob'; 'Zip'; 'Hippy Hippy Shake'; 'Jeans'; 'Siker Delick'; 'Pepsi'; 'Alphabetti Spaghetti'; 'Lounge Suite'; 'Fab'; 'Jacuzzi'; 'Big Mac'; 'Rice Krispies'; 'Work-Top'; 'The Twist'; 'Women's Lib'; and 'Jog'? Precious few, I could guess. But that still leaves us with the enigma of 'naff'. Might it possibly be a misprint for 'daff', meaning 'daffodil', and, if so, could Mr Cecil Parkinson rightly be described as 'a bit daffodil'? The cap fits, I think, but I look forward to a lively correspondence.

APPENDIX A

Placements at the Punch Lunch, June 5th 1970 (see pages 16-17):

Mr William Davie

Miss Wendy Craig	Miss Noele Gordon
Mr Woodrow Wyatt	Sir Gerald Nabarro MP
Quintin Hogg MP	Miss Maureen Lipmann
Mr Martin Amis	Mr Roy Hudd
Babs, Dabs and	Mr Terence Scott
Dibs Beverley	
Mr Jon Pertwee	Mr Roy Hattersley MP
Mr Michael Parkinson	HRH Princess Anne

Mr Wallace Arnold

APPENDIX B

From a speech delivered by HRH The Duke of Edinburgh at the Variety Club of Great Britain Luncheon to honour Wallace Arnold as King Water Rat, held at the Savoy Hotel, London, on May 23rd 1979:

'Mr Chief Barker, Ladies and Gentlement: Where to begin? I've always found it a sound rule over the course of a long and busy life to begin, not at the end, or even in the middle, but at the beginning. (*Laughter*)

'Wallace Arnold is, to my mind, one of those unique people who have brightened our lives in so many ways. Whether taking a wry – but never cruel – look at the comedy of human foibles for *Punch* magazine, or allowing us to glimpse his more concerned side in *The Spectacle* magazine, he is rightly regarded as the doyen of British scriveners.

'But the pen is not his only hat. He contributes much to the worlds of politics and the arts and – though I know he'll kick me for telling you this! – he is an ardent charity fundraiser. Only this morning, he tells me, he has donated no less than five framed photographs of himself, fully autographed, for an auction to raise funds for The Queen Mother's Eightieth Birthday Celebrations. (*Stunned silence followed by applause*)

'Wallace is also, he tells me, very much a People Person, and those assembled here today bear testament to the man's great talent for friendship with people less fortunate, perhaps, than himself. Please welcome, then, from the world of entertainment Miss Anita Harris (*applause*), from the world of politics, Mr John Moore (*applause*) and from the world of letters, Mr Timothy Rice (*applause*).

'Like so many prominent men, Wallace has that marvellous ability to laugh at himself. He tells the following anecdote at his own expense: one day, he entered a favourite restaurant where there was a new waiter – no doubt from Timbuctoo! – who failed to recognise him. In response to Wallace's complaint, the manager – a great admirer – replied, 'You are so distinguished-looking, Mr Arnold, that he must have taken you for Royalty!' To which Wallace replied – as quick as a flash – "One day, dear boy, one day!" (*laughter and applause*)

'Mr Chief Barker, Ladies and Gentlemen – I give you Mr Wallace Arnold.' (*Prolonged applause*)

APPENDIX C

Further Reading

Apart from Arnold's own works, many of them mentioned in the text, the following memoirs, reflections and critical studies may prove useful:

Acton, Harold. *Of Wisteria, Winter Blossom and Wallace Arnold: Poems by Harold Acton 1981-87*, (16pp, Arnold Press, 1990)

Beaton, Cecil. *The Wallace Years, Diaries 1963-74*. (350pp, Weidenfeld and Nicolson, 1978)

Cowlins, Maurice (ed.). *To Those That Have: The Economic Theory of Arnold. An Introduction*. (654pp, OUP, 1983)

Davis, William (ed.). *Pardon My Jests! The Punch Book of Wallace Arnold*. (190pp, Robson Books, 1972)

Greene, Graham. *Getting to Know Wallace Arnold* – (330pp, Bodley Head, 1986)

Noriega, Manuel. *The Garrick Years*. (229pp, André Deutsch, 1985)

Norwich, John Julius (ed.). *Never Sup Soup With A Fork!: The Aphorisms of Wallace Arnold*. (143pp, Chatto and Windus, 1974).

Skelton, Barbara. *All Man: My Years with Wallace Arnold*. (222pp, Hamish Hamilton, 1990)

Worsthorne, Terry (ed.). *Greetings Cher Maître! A Festschrift for Wallace Arnold*. Contributors include: Lord Hailsham, Peter Palumbo, Sir Roymond Strong, Ann Wilson, etc. Foreword by HRH The Duke of Edinburgh. All proceeds to Elocution for the Underprivileged. (160pp, Collins, 1978).